rjgrune.com

thanks for reading.

Galatians: Selections from Martin Luther's Commentary

ISBN-13: 978-0692429815 (rjgrune.com publishing)
ISBN-10: 0692429816

Title: Commentary on the Epistle to the Galatians
Year: 1535
Author: Martin Luther
Translator: Theodore Graebner
Language: English

From Luther's Introduction, 1538

In my heart reigns this one article, faith in my dear Lord Christ, the beginning, middle and end of whatever spiritual and divine thoughts I may have, whether by day or by night.

Contents

Introduction

Martin Luther is a theologian who has changed my life. Initially, he changed my life without me ever realizing it since I was baptized and raised in a Lutheran church. As I've grown in my faith and am now a preacher and teacher, I've continued to be influenced through the writings and teachings that have been passed on from Luther.

Luther, in a day when the Church hijacked the message of the Gospel, stood boldly for the proclamation of Christ alone. In a world that literally sold people forgiveness for a few bucks, Martin Luther came onto the scene recovering the message of the scriptures that said, "The price has already been paid."

But here's the thing about Luther. He wrote a ton and now that we are about 500 years out from his writing (not to mention it was written in a different language), it can be a bit tough to dive into the works of Luther.

Luther himself said about this commentary:

> *"I myself can hardly believe that I was so verbose as this book shows when I publicly expounded this letter of St. Paul to the Galatians. However, I can see that all the thoughts that I find in this treatise are mine, so I must confess that I uttered all of them, or perhaps more than all of them. The one article of faith that I have most at heart is the faith of Christ." - Martin Luther, Commentary on Galatians, Crossway Classic Series*

This leads to why I'm releasing this book. I think everybody should read Martin Luther. But his works can be intimidating. The goal of this book is to make Luther less intimidating. And there is no better place to start than Galatians, which is arguably one of Luther's best works.

What We Did With Luther

There are a couple of things that you can expect here that I think will make this a great introduction to Luther.

First, it's not the entire commentary on Galatians. The entire commentary is incredible and you should read it, but I have a feeling that the entire commentary will be a bit much for a lot of the people that I talk to.

Second, I've tried to divide it up in a way that fits how I'd want to read a book. The scriptures that Luther is referencing is within the text in an easy-to-read way and the text is broken up with headings and chapters that will make it easily scannable.

Third, art accompanies the text. Luther's theology and writing is incredible, I want the art and design of this book to reflect that. As you're reading, I want you to be able to stop and pause as certain phrases are called out with art.

Fourth, it's truly Luther. I'm not changing Luther's words. So when you read the commentary, it is truly the words of Luther as translated by Theodore Graebner. I've taken parts out but I didn't change the style of his language itself.

So how would I describe this book? It's Luther, but for everyday life. It brings a work that was written hundreds of years ago and remains relevant in our day and puts it in a package that is accessible for the average person.

If you're ready to skip my introduction, feel free to jump right into Luther's words in Chapter 1.

The Two Kinds of Righteousness

In the commentary on Galatians, Luther helps us get our categories straight.

He makes sure we don't muddy the waters of our theology by confusing Law and Gospel. He encourages us to understand the proper place of faith and works when he describes two kinds of righteousness. Luther, throughout his commentary on Galatians and throughout all of his work, does everything he can to make clear the forgiveness of sins. He reflects on the problems with the "foolish Galatians" and sees the same problems in the world he lives in.

When it comes to the righteousness we have before God, it rests solely on the work of Christ. Jesus declared, "It is finished." Martin Luther described us as "beggars." We are completely passive in our relationship with God, powerless to do what only God can do.

Passive righteousness is the vertical relationship between God and man. God does the work. The only contribution that man brings into this equation is sin. This is why Romans says, "No one is righteous - not even one."

When it is said that God doesn't need our good works, we can continue by saying, "but our neighbor does."

In our horizontal relationships, our righteousness is not passive, it is active. We not only have relationship with our Creator (passively), but we also have relationships with our neighbors. In our relationships with the world around us, God calls us to be active serving the world around us.

Active righteousness is what we do in our communities, our neighborhoods, our families, and our jobs. Active righteousness is where we fulfill our God-given vocations.

If we confuse the two and think that active righteousness establishes our relationship with God, we will trust in ourselves for salvation. Instead of relying solely on God in the vertical relationship, we will find ourselves relying on our own ability to follow the commandments or serve our neighbors.

If we confuse the two and think that passive righteousness carries over from our vertical relationship into our horizontal relationships, we will end up ignoring the needs of our neighbors. When we ignore active righteousness, we ignore our callings to our family, to our communities, and in our careers.

Instead we must see these two kind of righteousness clearly. In our relationship with God, we are recipients. We, like beggars, receive the gifts that only God can give. And in relationship with the world, we actively seek to do good and serve our neighbors.

This is why Luther writes:

> "Without any merit or work of our own, we must first be justified by Christian righteousness, which has nothing to do with the righteousness of the Law or with earthly and active righteousness. But this righteousness is heavenly and passive. We do not have it of ourselves; we receive it from heaven. We do not perform it; we accept it by faith, through which we ascend beyond all laws and works." - Martin Luther, Luther's Works, Vol. 26: Lectures on Galatians, CPH

And for the same reason he continues:

> "When I have this righteousness within me, I descend from heaven like the rain that makes the earth fertile. That is, I come forth into another kingdom, and I perform good works whenever the opportunity arises. If I am a minister of the Word, I preach, I comfort the saddened, I administer the sacraments. If I am a father, I rule my household and family, I train my children in piety and honesty. If I am a magistrate, I perform the office which I have received by divine command. If I am a servant, I faithfully tend to my master's affairs. In short, whoever knows for sure that Christ is his righteousness not only cheerfully and gladly works in his calling but also submits himself for the sake of love to magistrates, also to their wicked laws, and to everything else in this present life." - Martin Luther, Luther's Works, Vol. 26: Lectures on Galatians, CPH

I believe good theology isn't meant to be reserved for the academics and dead guys. Theology is for everyday life. My prayer in all of my writing and teaching is that the theology you read and hear won't be just for your "church life" but it will affect your life when you go to work on Monday morning.

My prayer for you as you dive into the work of Luther, specifically in his commentary on the book of Galatians, is that the grace of God will give you peace in the midst of a world that says "do more" and "try harder."

Grace & Peace,

RJ Grunewald
rjgrune.com

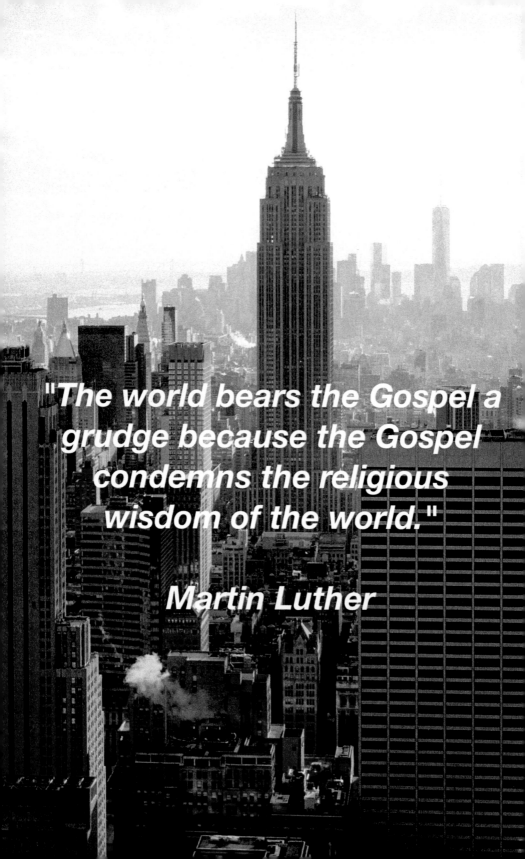

"The world bears the Gospel a grudge because the Gospel condemns the religious wisdom of the world."

Martin Luther

Grace and Peace
Chapter 1

Paul, an apostle—not from men nor through man, but through Jesus Christ and God the Father, who raised him from the dead— and all the brothers who are with me,

To the churches of Galatia:

Grace to you and peace from God our Father and the Lord Jesus Christ, who gave himself for our sins to deliver us from the present evil age, according to the will of our God and Father, to whom be the glory forever and ever. Amen. - Galatians 1:1-5 (ESV)

St. Paul wrote this epistle because, after his departure from the Galatian churches, Jewish-Christian fanatics moved in, who perverted Paul's Gospel of man's free justification by faith in Christ Jesus.

The world bears the Gospel a grudge because the Gospel condemns the religious wisdom of the world. Jealous for its own religious views, the world in turn charges the Gospel with being a subversive and licentious doctrine, offensive to God and man, a doctrine to be persecuted as the worst plague on earth.

As a result we have this paradoxical situation: The Gospel supplies the world with the salvation of Jesus Christ, peace of conscience, and every blessing. Just for that the world abhors the Gospel.

Grace and Peace
The terms of grace and peace are common terms with Paul and are now pretty well understood. But since we are explaining this epistle, you will not mind if we repeat what we have so often explained elsewhere. The article of justification must be sounded in our ears incessantly because the frailty of our flesh will not permit us to take hold of it perfectly and to believe it with all our heart.

The greeting of the Apostle is refreshing.

Grace remits sin, and peace quiets the conscience. Sin and conscience torment us, but Christ has overcome these fiends now and forever. Only Christians possess this victorious knowledge given from above. These two terms, grace and peace, constitute Christianity. Grace involves the remission of sins, peace, and a happy conscience. Sin is not canceled by lawful living, for no person is able to live up to the Law. The Law reveals guilt, fills the conscience with terror, and drives men to despair. Much less is sin taken away by man-invented endeavors. The fact is, the more a person seeks credit for himself by his own efforts, the deeper he goes into debt. Nothing can take away sin except the grace of God. In actual living, however, it is not so easy to persuade oneself that by grace alone, in opposition to every other means, we obtain the forgiveness of our sins and peace with God.

The world brands this a pernicious doctrine. The world advances free will, the rational and natural approach of good works, as the means of obtaining the forgiveness of sin. But it is impossible to gain peace of conscience by the methods and means of the world. Experience proves this. Various holy orders have been launched for the purpose of securing peace of conscience through religious exercises, but they proved failures because such devices only increase doubt and despair. We find no rest for our weary bones unless we cling to the word of grace.

The Apostle does not wish the Galatians grace and peace from the emperor, or from kings, or from governors, but from God the Father. He wishes them heavenly peace, the kind of which Jesus spoke when He said, "Peace I leave unto you: my peace I give unto you." Worldly peace provides quiet enjoyment of life and possessions. But in affliction, particularly in the hour of death, the grace and peace of the world will not deliver us. However, the grace and peace of God will. They make a person strong and courageous to bear and to overcome all difficulties, even death itself, because we have the victory of Christ's death and the assurance of the forgiveness of our sins.

Sin is an exacting despot who can
be vanquished by no created power,
but by the sovereign power of Jesus Christ alone.

For Our Sins

Paul sticks to his theme.

He never loses sight of the purpose of his epistle. He does not say, "Who received our works," but "who gave." Gave what? Not gold, or silver, or paschal lambs, or an angel, but Himself. What for? Not for a crown, or a kingdom, or our goodness, but for our sins. These words are like so many thunderclaps of protest from heaven against every kind and type of self-merit. Underscore these words, for they are full of comfort for sore consciences.

How may we obtain remission of our sins?

Paul answers: "The man who is named Jesus Christ and the Son of God gave himself for our sins." The heavy artillery of these words explodes papacy, works, merits, superstitions. For if our sins could be removed by our own efforts, what need was there for the Son of God to be given for them? Since Christ was given for our sins it stands to reason that they cannot be put away by our own efforts.

This sentence also defines our sins as great, so great, in fact, that the whole world could not make amends for a single sin. The greatness of the ransom, Christ, the Son of God, indicates this. The vicious character of sin is brought out by the words "who gave himself for our sins." So vicious is sin that only the sacrifice of Christ could atone for sin. When we reflect that the one little word "sin" embraces the whole kingdom of Satan, and that it includes everything that is horrible, we have reason to tremble. But we are careless. We make light of sin. We think that by some little work or merit we can dismiss sin.

This passage, then, bears out the fact that all men are sold under sin. Sin is an exacting despot who can be vanquished by no created power, but by the sovereign power of Jesus Christ alone.

All this is of wonderful comfort to a conscience troubled by the enormity of sin. Sin cannot harm those who believe in Christ, because He has overcome sin by His death. Armed with this conviction, we are enlightened and may pass judgment upon the papists, monks, nuns, priests, Mohammedans, Anabaptists, and all who trust in their own merits, as wicked and destructive sects that rob God and Christ of the honor that belongs to them alone.

Note especially the pronoun "our" and its significance. You will readily grant that Christ gave Himself for the sins of Peter, Paul, and others who were worthy of such grace. But feeling low, you find it hard to believe that Christ gave Himself for your sins. Our feelings shy at a personal application of the pronoun "our" and we refuse to have anything to do with God until we have made ourselves worthy by good deeds.

This attitude springs from a false conception of sin, the conception that sin is a small matter, easily taken care of by good works; that we must present ourselves unto God with a good conscience; that we must feel no sin before we may feel that Christ was given for our sins.

This attitude is universal and particularly developed in those who consider themselves better than others. Such readily confess that they are frequent sinners, but they regard their sins as of no such importance that they cannot easily be dissolved by some good action, or that they may not appear before the tribunal of Christ and demand the reward of eternal life for their righteousness. Meantime they pretend great humility and acknowledge a certain degree of sinfulness for which they soulfully join in the publican's prayer, "God be merciful to me a sinner." But the real significance and comfort of the words "for our sins" is lost upon them.

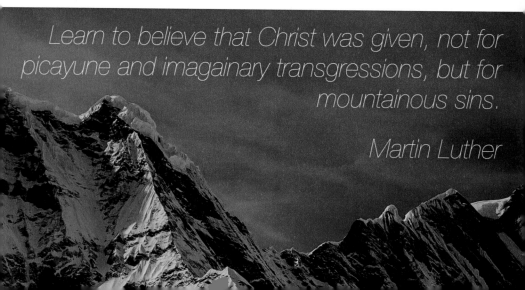

Learn to believe that Christ was given, not for picayune and imagainary transgressions, but for mountainous sins.

Martin Luther

The genius of Christianity takes the words of Paul "who gave himself for our sins" as true and efficacious. We are not to look upon our sins as insignificant trifles. On the other hand, we are not to regard them as so terrible that we must despair. Learn to believe that Christ was given, not for picayune and imaginary transgressions, but for mountainous sins; not for one or two, but for all; not for sins that can be discarded, but for sins that are stubbornly ingrained.

> *I am astonished that you are so quickly deserting him who called you in the grace of Christ and are turning to a different gospel — not that there is another one, but there are some who trouble you and want to distort the gospel of Christ. But even if we or an angel from heaven should preach to you a gospel contrary to the one we preached to you, let him be accursed. As we have said before, so now I say again: If anyone is preaching to you a gospel contrary to the one you received, let him be accursed.*
>
> *For am I now seeking the approval of man, or of God? Or am I trying to please man? If I were still trying to please man, I would not be a servant of Christ. - Galatians 1:6-10 (ESV)*

How patiently Paul deals with his seduced Galatians!

He does not pounce on them but, like a father, he fairly excuses their error. With motherly affection he talks to them yet he does it in a way that at the same time he also reproves them. On the other hand, he is highly indignant at the seducers whom he blames for the apostasy of the Galatians. His anger bursts forth in elemental fury at the beginning of his epistle. "If any may," he cries, "preach any other gospel unto you than that ye have received, let him be accursed." Later on, in the fifth chapter, he threatens the false apostles with damnation. "He that troubleth you shall bear his judgment, whosoever he be." He pronounces a curse upon them. "I would they were even cut off which trouble you."

Paul deplores the fact that it is difficult for the mind to retain a sound and steadfast faith. A man labors for a decade before he succeeds in training his little church into orderly religion, and then some ignorant and vicious poltroon comes along to overthrow in a minute the patient labor of years. By the grace of God we have effected here in Wittenberg the form of a Christian church. The Word of God is taught as it should be, the Sacraments are administered, and everything is prosperous. This happy condition, secured by many years of arduous labors, some lunatic might spoil in a moment. This happened in the churches of Galatia which Paul had brought into life in spiritual travail. Soon after his departure, however, these Galatian churches were thrown into confusion by the false apostles.

The church is a tender plant. It must be watched. People hear a couple of sermons, scan a few pages of Holy Writ, and think they know it all. They are bold because they have never gone through any trials of faith. Void of the Holy Spirit, they teach what they please as long as it sounds good to the common people who are ever ready to join something new.

Why does the world abhor the glad tidings of the Gospel and the blessings that go with it? Because the world is the devil's. Under his direction the world persecutes the Gospel and would if it could nail again Christ, the Son of God, to the Cross although He gave Himself into death for the sins of the world. The world dwells in darkness. The world is darkness.

Paul accentuates the point that the Galatians had been called by Christ unto grace. "I taught you the doctrine of grace and of liberty from the Law, from sin and wrath, that you should be free in Christ, and not slaves to the hard laws of Moses. Will you allow yourselves to be carried away so easily from the living fountain of grace and life?"

A Different Gospel

To paraphrase: "These false apostles do not merely trouble you, they abolish Christ's Gospel. They act as if they were the only true Gospel-preachers. For all that they muddle Law and Gospel. As a result they pervert the Gospel. Either Christ must live and the Law perish, or the Law remains and Christ must perish; Christ and the Law cannot dwell side by side in the conscience. It is either grace or law. To muddle the two is to eliminate the Gospel of Christ entirely."

It seems a small matter to mingle the Law and Gospel, faith and works, but it creates more mischief than man's brain can conceive. To mix Law and Gospel not only clouds the knowledge of grace, it cuts out Christ altogether.

The words of Paul, "and would pervert the gospel of Christ," also indicate how arrogant these false apostles were. They were shameless boasters. Paul simply had to exalt his own ministry and Gospel. Paul maintains that there is no other gospel besides the one he had preached to the Galatians. He preached, not a gospel of his own invention, but the very same Gospel God had long ago prescribed in the Sacred Scriptures.

For I would have you know, brothers, that the gospel that was preached by me is not man's gospel. For I did not receive it from any man, nor was I taught it, but I received it through a revelation of Jesus Christ. For you have heard of my former life in Judaism, how I persecuted the church of God violently and tried to destroy it. And I was advancing in Judaism beyond many of my own age among my people, so extremely zealous was I for the traditions of my fathers. But when he who had set me apart before I was born, and who called me by his grace, was pleased to reveal his Son to me, in order that I might preach him among the Gentiles, I did not immediately consult with anyone; nor did I go up to Jerusalem to those who were apostles before me, but I went away into Arabia, and returned again to Damascus.

Then after three years I went up to Jerusalem to visit Cephas and remained with him fifteen days. But I saw none of the other apostles except James the Lord's brother. (In what I am writing to you, before God, I do not lie!) Then I went into the regions of Syria and Cilicia. And I was still unknown in person to the churches of Judea that are in Christ. They only were hearing it said, "He who used to persecute us is now preaching the faith he once tried to destroy." And they glorified God because of me. - Galatians 1:11-24 (ESV)

This passage constitutes Paul's chief defense against the accusations of his opponents. He maintains under oath that he received his Gospel not from men, but by the revelation of Jesus Christ.

Paul received his Gospel on the way to Damascus when Christ appeared to him. St. Luke furnishes an account of the incident in the ninth chapter of the Book of Acts. "Arise," said Christ to Paul, "and go into the city, and it shall be told thee what thou must do." Christ did not send Paul into the city to learn the Gospel from Ananias. Ananias was only to baptize Paul, to lay his hands on Paul, to commit the ministry of the Word unto Paul, and to recommend him to the Church. Ananias recognized his limited assignment when he said to Paul: "Brother Saul, the Lord, even Jesus, that appeared unto thee in the way as thou camest, hath sent me, that thou mightest receive thy sight, and be filled with the Holy Ghost." Paul did not receive instruction from Ananias. Paul had already been called, enlightened, and taught by Christ in the road. His contact with Ananias was merely a testimonial to the fact that Paul had been called by Christ to preach the Gospel.

Paul was forced to speak of his conversion to combat the slanderous contention of the false apostles to the effect that this apostleship was inferior to that of the other apostles.

Forfeiting the Gospel

The article of justification is fragile. Not in itself, of course, but in us. I know how quickly a person can forfeit the joy of the Gospel. I know in what slippery places even those stand who seem to have a good footing in the matters of faith. In the midst of the conflict when we should be consoling ourselves with the Gospel, the Law rears up and begins to rage all over our conscience. I say the Gospel is frail because we are frail.

The article of justification is fragile.

What makes matters worse is that one-half of ourselves, our own reason, stands against us. The flesh resists the spirit, or as Paul puts it, "The flesh lusteth against the Spirit." Therefore we teach that to know Christ and to believe in Him is no achievement of man, but the gift of God. God alone can create and preserve faith in us. God creates faith in us through the Word. He increases, strengthens and confirms faith in us through His word. Hence the best service that anybody can render God is diligently to hear and read God's Word. On the other hand, nothing is more perilous than to be weary of the Word of God. Thinking he knows enough, a person begins little by little to despise the Word until he has lost Christ and the Gospel altogether.

Let every believer carefully learn the Gospel. Let him continue in humble prayer. We are molested not by puny foes, but by mighty ones, foes who never grow tired of warring against us. These, our enemies, are many: Our own flesh, the world, the Law, sin, death, the wrath and judgment of God, and the devil himself.

"So extremely zealous was I for the traditions of my fathers…"

Speaking now of the Mosaic Law, Paul declares that he was wrapped up in it.

"When it had pleased God," he writes, "I did not deserve it. I had been an enemy of Christ. I had blasphemed His Gospel. I had shed innocent blood. In the midst of my frenzy I was called. Why? On account of my outrageous cruelty? Indeed not. My gracious God who shows mercy unto whom He will, pardoned all mine iniquities. He bestowed His grace upon me, and called me for an apostle."

We also have come to the knowledge of the truth by the same kindness of God.

I crucified Christ daily in my cloistered life, and blasphemed God by my wrong faith. Outwardly I kept myself chaste, poor, and obedient. I was much given to fasting, watching, praying, saying of masses, and the like. Yet under the cloak of my outward respectability I continually mistrusted, doubted, feared, hated, and blasphemed God. My righteousness was a filthy puddle. Satan loves such saints. They are his darlings, for they quickly destroy their body and soul by depriving them of the blessings of God's generous gifts.

"Did God call me on account of my holy life? Or on account of my pharisaical religion? Or on account of my prayers, fastings, and works?

Never.

The Gospel does not threaten.

The Gospel announces that Christ
is come to forgive the sins of the world.

Well, then, it is certain God did not call me on account of my blasphemies, persecutions, oppressions. What prompted Him to call me? His grace alone."

We now hear what kind of doctrine was committed to Paul: The doctrine of the Gospel, the doctrine of the revelation of the Son of God. This doctrine differs greatly from the Law. The Law terrorizes the conscience. The Law reveals the wrath and judgment of God. The Gospel does not threaten. The Gospel announces that Christ is come to forgive the sins of the world. The Gospel conveys to us the inestimable treasures of God.

Christ is no sheriff.
He is "the Lamb of God,
which taketh away
the sin of the world."

Martin Luther

For Me
Chapter 2

Then after fourteen years I went up again to Jerusalem with Barnabas, taking Titus along with me. I went up because of a revelation and set before them (though privately before those who seemed influential) the gospel that I proclaim among the Gentiles, in order to make sure I was not running or had not run in vain. But even Titus, who was with me, was not forced to be circumcised, though he was a Greek. Yet because of false brothers secretly brought in—who slipped in to spy out our freedom that we have in Christ Jesus, so that they might bring us into slavery— to them we did not yield in submission even for a moment, so that the truth of the gospel might be preserved for you. - Galatians 2:1-5 (ESV)

When Paul speaks of the truth of the Gospel he implies by contrast a false gospel. The false apostles also had a gospel, but it was an untrue gospel.

Now the true Gospel has it that we are justified by faith alone, without the deeds of the Law. The false gospel has it that we are justified by faith, but not without the deeds of the Law. The false apostles preached a conditional gospel.

They admit that faith is the foundation of salvation. But they add the conditional clause that faith can save only when it is furnished with good works.

This is wrong.

The true Gospel declares that good works are the embellishment of faith, but that faith itself is the gift and work of God in our hearts. Faith is able to justify, because it apprehends Christ, the Redeemer.

Human reason can think only in terms of the Law. It mumbles: "This I have done, this I have not done." But faith looks to Jesus Christ, the Son of God, given into death for the sins of the whole world. To turn one's eyes away from Jesus means to turn them to the Law.

True faith lays hold of Christ and leans on Him alone. Our opponents cannot understand this. In their blindness they cast away the precious pearl, Christ, and hang onto their stubborn works. They have no idea what faith is. How can they teach faith to others?

> *When Cephas came to Antioch, I opposed him to his face, because he stood condemned. For before certain men came from James, he used to eat with the Gentiles. But when they arrived, he began to draw back and separate himself from the Gentiles because he was afraid of those who belonged to the circumcision group. The other Jews joined him in his hypocrisy, so that by their hypocrisy even Barnabas was led astray.*
>
> *When I saw that they were not acting in line with the truth of the gospel, I said to Cephas in front of them all, "You are a Jew, yet you live like a Gentile and not like a Jew. How is it, then, that you force Gentiles to follow Jewish customs? - Galatians 2:11-14 (NIV)*

Paul accuses the false apostles of slandering him behind his back. In his presence they dared not to open their mouths. He tells them, "I did not speak evil of Peter behind his back, but I withstood him frankly and openly."

Others may debate here whether an apostle might sin. I claim that we ought not to make Peter out as faultless. Prophets have erred. Nathan told David that he should go ahead and build the Temple of the Lord. But his prophecy was afterwards corrected by the Lord. The apostles erred in thinking of the Kingdom of Christ as a worldly state. Peter had heard the command of Christ, "Go ye into all the world, and preach the Gospel to every creature." But if it had not been for the heavenly vision and the special command of Christ, Peter would never have gone to the home of Cornelius. Peter also erred in this matter of circumcision. If Paul had not publicly censured him, all the believing Gentiles would have been compelled to receive circumcision and accept the Jewish law. We are not to attribute perfection to any man.

Luke reports "that the contention between Paul and Barnabas was so sharp that they departed asunder one from the other." The cause of their disagreement could hardly have been small since it separated these two, who had been joined together for years in a holy partnership. Such incidents are recorded for our consolation. After all, it is a comfort to know that even saints might and do sin.

Samson, David, and many other excellent men, fell into grievous sins. Job and Jeremiah cursed the day of their birth. Elijah and Jonah became weary of life and prayed for death. Such offenses on the part of the saints, the Scriptures record for the comfort of those who are near despair. No person has ever sunk so low that he cannot rise again. On the other hand, no man's standing is so secure that he may not fall. If Peter fell, I may fall. If he rose again, I may rise again. We have the same gifts that they had, the same Christ, the same baptism and the same Gospel, the same forgiveness of sins. They needed these saving ordinances just as much as we do.

> *When the conscience is disturbed,*
> *do not seek advice from reason or from the Law,*
> *but rest your conscience*
> *in the grace of God and in His Word.*

Dividing Law & Gospel

When it come to the article of justification we must not yield, if we want to retain the truth of the Gospel. When the conscience is disturbed, do not seek advice from reason or from the Law, but rest your conscience in the grace of God and in His Word, and proceed as if you had never heard of the Law. The Law has its place and its own good time.

The person who can rightly divide Law and Gospel has reason to thank God. He is a true theologian. I must confess that in times of temptation I do not always know how to do it. To divide Law and Gospel means to place the Gospel in heaven, and to keep the Law on earth; to call the righteousness of the Gospel heavenly, and the righteousness of the Law earthly; to put as much difference between the righteousness of the Gospel and that of the Law, as there is difference between day and night. If it is a question of faith or conscience, ignore the Law entirely. If it is a question of works, then lift high the lantern of works and the righteousness of the Law. If your conscience is oppressed with a sense of sin, talk to your conscience. Say: "You are now groveling in the dirt. You are now a laboring ass. Go ahead, and carry your burden. But why don't you mount up to heaven? There the Law cannot follow you!" Leave the ass burdened with laws behind in the valley.

By his compromising attitude Peter confused the separation of Law and Gospel. Paul had to do something about it. He reproved Peter, not to embarrass him, but to conserve the difference between the Gospel which justifies in heaven, and the Law which justifies on earth.

The right separation between Law and Gospel is very important to know. Christian doctrine is impossible without it. Let all who love and fear God, diligently learn the difference, not only in theory but also in practice.

When your conscience gets into trouble, say to yourself: "There is a time to die, and a time to live; a time to learn the Law, and a time to unlearn the Law; a time to hear the Gospel, and a time to ignore the Gospel. Let the Law now depart, and let the Gospel enter, for now is the right time to hear the Gospel, and not the Law." However, when the conflict of conscience is over and external duties must be performed, close your ears to the Gospel, and open them wide to the Law.

"We who are Jews by birth and not sinful Gentiles know that a person is not justified by the works of the law, but by faith in Jesus Christ. So we, too, have put our faith in Christ Jesus that we may be justified by faith in Christ and not by the works of the law, because by the works of the law no one will be justified.

"But if, in seeking to be justified in Christ, we Jews find ourselves also among the sinners, doesn't that mean that Christ promotes sin? Absolutely not! If I rebuild what I destroyed, then I really would be a lawbreaker.

"For through the law I died to the law so that I might live for God. I have been crucified with Christ and I no longer live, but Christ lives in

me. The life I now live in the body, I live by faith in the Son of God, who loved me and gave himself for me. I do not set aside the grace of God, for if righteousness could be gained through the law, Christ died for nothing!" - Galatians 2:15-21 (NIV)

Having been humbled by the Law, and having been brought to a right estimate of himself, a man will repent. He finds out that he is so depraved, that no strength, no works, no merits of his own will ever deliver him from his guilt. He will then understand the meaning of Paul's words: "I am sold under sin"; and "they are all under sin."

At this state a person begins to lament: "Who is going to help me?" In due time comes the Word of the Gospel, and says: "Son, thy sins are forgiven thee. Believe in Jesus Christ who was crucified for your sins. Remember, your sins have been imposed upon Christ."

In this way are we delivered from sin. In this way are we justified and made heirs of everlasting life.

In order to have faith you must paint a true portrait of Christ. The scholastics caricature Christ into a judge and tormentor. But Christ is no law giver. He is the Life giver. He is the Forgiver of sins. You must believe that Christ might have atoned for the sins of the world with one single drop of His blood. Instead, He shed His blood abundantly in order that He might give abundant satisfaction for our sins.

Here let me say, that these three things, faith, Christ, and imputation of righteousness, are to be joined together. Faith takes hold of Christ. God accounts this faith for righteousness.

This imputation of righteousness we need very much, because we are far from perfect. As long as we have this body, sin will dwell in our flesh. Then, too, we sometimes drive away the Holy Spirit; we fall into sin, like Peter, David, and other holy men. Nevertheless we may always take recourse to this fact, "that our sins are covered," and that "God will not lay them to our charge." Sin is not held against us for Christ's sake. Where Christ and faith are lacking, there is no remission or covering of sins, but only condemnation.

Works Flowing From Forgiveness

After we have taught faith in Christ, we teach good works. "Since you have found Christ by faith," we say, "begin now to work and do well. Love God and your neighbor. Call upon God, give thanks unto Him, praise Him, confess Him. These are good works. Let them flow from a cheerful heart, because you have remission of sin in Christ."

When crosses and afflictions come our way, we bear them patiently. "For Christ's yoke is easy, and His burden is light." When sin has been pardoned, and the conscience has been eased of its dreadful load, a Christian can endure all things in Christ.

To give a short definition of a Christian: A Christian is not somebody who chalks sin, because of his faith in Christ. This doctrine brings comfort to consciences in serious trouble. When a person is a Christian he is above law and sin. When the Law accuses him, and sin wants to drive the wits out of him, a Christian looks to Christ. A Christian is free. He has no master except Christ. A Christian is greater than the whole world.

The Law is a good thing. But when the discussion is about justification, then is no time to drag in the Law. When we discuss justification we ought to speak of Christ and the benefits He has brought us.

Christ is no sheriff. He is "the Lamb of God, which taketh away the sin of the world." (John 1:29.)

By the grace of God we know that we are justified through faith in Christ alone. We do not mingle law and grace, faith and works. We keep them far apart. Let every true Christian mark the distinction between law and grace, and mark it well.

The Law is a good thing.
But when the discussion is about justification,
then is no time to drag in the Law.

"For through the law I died to the law, so that I might live to God."

This nineteenth verse is loaded with consolation. It fortifies a person against every danger. It allows you to argue like this:

"I confess I have sinned." "Then God will punish you." "No, He will not do that." "Why not? Does not the Law say so?" "I have nothing to do with the Law." "How so?" "I have another law, the law of liberty." "What do you mean--'liberty'?" "The liberty of Christ, for Christ has made me free from the Law that held me down. That Law is now in prison itself, held captive by grace and liberty."

By faith in Christ a person may gain such sure and sound comfort, that he need not fear the devil, sin, death, or any evil.

What is righteousness?
Paul explains what constitutes true Christian righteousness. True Christian righteousness is the righteousness of Christ who lives in us. We must look away from our own person. Christ and my conscience must become one, so that I can see nothing else but Christ crucified and raised from the dead for me. If I keep on looking at myself, I am gone.

If we lose sight of Christ and begin to consider our past, we simply go to pieces. We must turn our eyes to the brazen serpent, Christ crucified, and believe with all our heart that He is our righteousness and our life. For Christ, on whom our eyes are fixed, in whom we live, who lives in us, is Lord over Law, sin, death, and all evil.

Faith connects you so intimately with Christ, that He and you become as it were one person. As such you may boldly say: "I am now one with Christ. Therefore Christ's righteousness, victory, and life are mine." On the other hand, Christ may say: "I am that big sinner. His sins and his death are mine, because he is joined to me, and I to him."

A Christian uses earthly means like any unbeliever. Outwardly they look alike. Nevertheless there is a great difference between them. I may live in the flesh, but I do not live after the flesh. I do my living now "by the faith of the Son of God." Paul had the same voice, the same tongue, before and after his conversion. Before his conversion his tongue uttered blasphemies. But after his conversion his tongue spoke a spiritual, heavenly language.

We may now understand how spiritual life originates. It enters the heart by faith. Christ reigns in the heart with His Holy Spirit, who sees, hears, speaks, works, suffers, and does all things in and through us over the protest and the resistance of the flesh.

For Me
Who is this "me"?

I, wretched and damnable sinner, dearly beloved of the Son of God. If I could by work or merit love the Son of God and come to Him, why should He have sacrificed Himself for me?

If I, a condemned sinner, could have been purchased and redeemed by any other price, why should the Son of God have given Himself for me? Just because there was no other price in heaven and on earth big and good enough, was it necessary for the Son of God to be delivered for me. This He did out of His great love for me, for the Apostle says, "Who loved me."

Did the Law ever love me?

Did the Law ever sacrifice itself for me?

Did the Law ever die for me?

On the contrary, it accuses me, it frightens me, it drives me crazy. Somebody else saved me from the Law, from sin and death unto eternal life. That Somebody is the Son of God, to whom be praise and glory forever.

For Christ is Joy and Sweetness to a broken heart. Christ is a Lover of poor sinners, and such a Lover that He gave Himself for us. Now if this is true, and it is true, then are we never justified by our own righteousness.

Read the words "me" and "for me" with great emphasis.

Print this "me" with capital letters in your heart, and do not ever doubt that you belong to the number of those who are meant by this "me." Christ did not only love Peter and Paul. The same love He felt for them He feels for us. If we cannot deny that we are sinners, we cannot deny that Christ died for our sins.

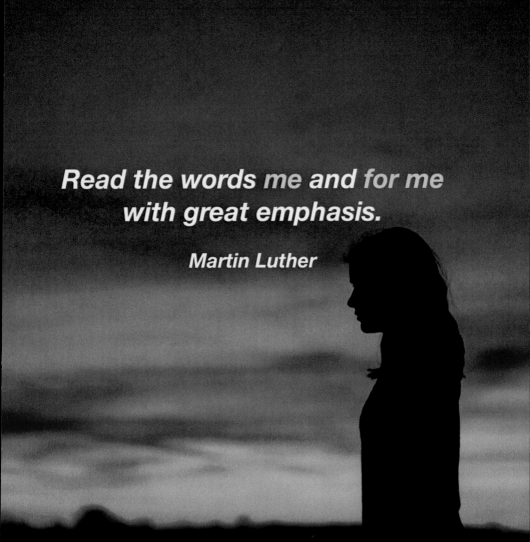

Read the words me and for me with great emphasis.

Martin Luther

*The Law bows a person down. It takes the **Gospel** and the preaching of **faith in Christ** to raise and save a person.*

Martin Luther

Foolish Galatians
Chapter 3

O foolish Galatians! Who has bewitched you? It was before your eyes that Jesus Christ was publicly portrayed as crucified. Let me ask you only this: Did you receive the Spirit by works of the law or by hearing with faith? Are you so foolish? Having begun by the Spirit, are you now being perfected by the flesh? Did you suffer so many things in vain —if indeed it was in vain? Does he who supplies the Spirit to you and works miracles among you do so by works of the law, or by hearing with faith— just as Abraham "believed God, and it was counted to him as righteousness"?

Know then that it is those of faith who are the sons of Abraham. And the Scripture, foreseeing that God would justify the Gentiles by faith, preached the gospel beforehand to Abraham, saying, "In you shall all the nations be blessed." So then, those who are of faith are blessed along with Abraham, the man of faith. - Galatians 3:1-9 (ESV)

The Apostle Paul manifests his apostolic care for the Galatians. Sometimes he entreats them, then again he reproaches them, in accordance with his own advice to Timothy: "Preach the word; be instant in season, out of season; reprove, rebuke, exhort."

In the midst of his discourse on Christian righteousness Paul breaks off, and turns to address the Galatians. "O foolish Galatians," he cries. "I have brought you the true Gospel, and you received it with eagerness and gratitude. Now all of a sudden you drop the Gospel. What has got into you?"

We have here an example of bad traits that often cling to individual Christians and entire congregations. Grace does not suddenly transform a Christian into a new and perfect creature. Dregs of the old and natural corruption remain. The Spirit of God cannot at once overcome human deficiency.

Sanctification takes time.

The apostasy of the Galatians is a fine endorsement of the Law, all right. You may preach the Law ever so fervently; if the preaching of the Gospel does not accompany it, the Law will never produce true conversion and heartfelt repentance. We do not mean to say that the preaching of the Law is without value, but it only serves to bring home to us the wrath of God. The Law bows a person down. It takes the Gospel and the preaching of faith in Christ to raise and save a person.

Paul's increasing severity becomes apparent as he reminds the Galatians that they disobeyed the truth in defiance of the vivid description he had given them of Christ. So vividly had he described Christ to them that they could almost see and handle Him. As if Paul were to say: "No artist with all his colors could have pictured Christ to you as vividly as I have pictured Him to you by my preaching. Yet you permitted yourselves to be seduced to the extent that you disobeyed the truth of Christ."

The Law Doesn't Produce Faith

Try to appreciate the force of Paul's argument which is so often repeated in the Book of Acts. That Book was written for the express purpose of verifying Paul's assertion, that the Holy Ghost comes upon men, not in response to the preaching of the Law, but in response to the preaching of the Gospel.

When Peter preached Christ at the first Pentecost, the Holy Ghost fell upon the hearers, "and the same day there were added unto them about three thousand souls." Cornelius received the Holy Ghost while Peter was speaking of Christ. "The Holy Ghost fell on all of them which heard the word." These are actual experiences that cannot very well be denied. When Paul and Barnabas returned to Jerusalem and reported what they had been able to accomplish among the Gentiles, the whole Church was astonished, particularly when it heard that the uncircumcised Gentiles had received the Holy Ghost by the preaching of faith in Christ.

Now as God gave the Holy Ghost to the Gentiles without the Law by the simple preaching of the Gospel, so He gave the Holy Ghost also to the Jews, without the Law, through faith alone. If the righteousness of the Law were necessary unto salvation, the Holy Ghost would never have come to the Gentiles, because they did not bother about the Law. Hence the Law does not justify, but faith in Christ justifies.

How was it with Cornelius? Cornelius and his friends whom he had invited over to his house, do nothing but sit and listen. Peter is doing the talking. They just sit and do nothing. The Law is far removed from their thoughts. They burn no sacrifices. They are not at all interested in circumcision. All they do is to sit and listen to Peter. Suddenly the Holy Ghost enters their hearts. His presence is unmistakable, "for they spoke with tongues and magnified God."

Right here we have one more difference between the Law and the Gospel.

The Law does not bring on the Holy Ghost. The Gospel, however, brings on the gift of the Holy Ghost, because it is the nature of the Gospel to convey good gifts. The Law and the Gospel are contrary ideas. They have contrary functions and purposes. To endow the Law with any capacity to produce righteousness is to plagiarize the Gospel. The Gospel brings donations. It pleads for open hands to take what is being offered. The Law has nothing to give. It demands, and its demands are impossible.

To endow the Law with any capacity to produce righteousness is to plagiarize the Gospel.

I have good reason for enlarging upon this point.

The heart of man finds it difficult to believe that so great a treasure as the Holy Ghost is gotten by the mere hearing of faith. The hearer likes to reason like this: Forgiveness of sins, deliverance from death, the gift of the Holy Ghost, everlasting life are grand things. If you want to obtain these priceless benefits, you must engage in correspondingly great efforts. And the devil says, "Amen."

We must learn that forgiveness of sins, Christ, and the Holy Ghost, are freely granted unto us at the preaching of faith, in spite of our sinfulness. We are not to waste time thinking how unworthy we are of the blessings of God. We are to know that it pleased God freely to give us His unspeakable gifts. If He offers His gifts free of charge, why not take them? Why worry about our lack of worthiness? Why not accept gifts with joy and thanksgiving?

Right away foolish reason is once more offended. It scolds us. "When you say that a person can do nothing to obtain the grace of God, you foster carnal security. People become shiftless and will do no good at all. Better not preach this doctrine of faith. Rather urge the people to exert and to exercise themselves in good works, so that the Holy Ghost will feel like coming to them."

A person becomes a Christian not by working, but by hearing. The first step to being a Christian is to hear the Gospel. When a person has accepted the Gospel, let him first give thanks unto God with a glad heart, and then let him get busy on the good works to strive for, works that really please God, and not man-made and self-chosen works.

God "winks" at my sins and covers them up. God says: "Because you believe in My Son I will forgive your sins until death shall deliver you from the body of sin."

Learn to understand the constitution of your Christian righteousness. Faith is weak, but it means enough to God that He will not lay sin to our charge. He will not punish nor condemn us for it. He will forgive our sins as though they amount to nothing at all. He will do it not because we are worthy of such mercy. He will do it for Jesus' sake in whom we believe.

Paradoxically, a Christian is both right and wrong, holy and profane, an enemy of God and a child of God. These contradictions no person can harmonize who does not understand the true way of salvation. Under the papacy we were told to toil until the feeling of guilt had left us. But the authors of this deranged idea were frequently driven to despair in the hour of death. It would have happened to me, if Christ had not mercifully delivered me from this error.

We comfort the afflicted sinner in this manner: Brother, you can never be perfect in this life, but you can be holy. He will say: "How can I be holy when I feel my sins?" I answer: You feel sin? That is a good sign. To realize that one is ill is a step, and a very necessary step, toward recovery. "But how will I get rid of my sin?" he will ask. I answer: See the heavenly Physician, Christ, who heals the broken-hearted. Do not consult that Quackdoctor, Reason. Believe in Christ and your sins will be pardoned. His righteousness will become your righteousness, and your sins will become His sins.

A Christian is beloved of God and a sinner. How can these two contradictions be harmonized: I am a sinner and deserve God's wrath and punishment, and yet the Father loves me? Christ alone can harmonize these contradictions. He is the Mediator.

> *For all who rely on works of the law are under a curse; for it is written, "Cursed be everyone who does not abide by all things written in the Book of the Law, and do them." Now it is evident that no one is justified before God by the law, for "The righteous shall live by faith." But the law is not of faith, rather "The one who does them shall live by them." Christ redeemed us from the curse of the law by becoming a curse for us —for it is written, "Cursed is everyone who is hanged on a tree"— so that in Christ Jesus the blessing of Abraham might come to the Gentiles, so that we might receive the promised Spirit through faith. - Galatians 3:10-14 (ESV)*

The curse of God is like a flood that swallows everything that is not of faith. To avoid the curse we must hold on to the promise of the blessing in Christ.

The scholastics admit that a mere external and superficial performance of the Law without sincerity and good will is plain hypocrisy. Judas acted like the other disciples. What was wrong with Judas? Mark what Rome answers, "Judas was a reprobate. His motives were perverse, therefore his works were hypocritical and no good."

The heart must be purified by faith before a person can lift a finger to please God.

There are two classes of doers of the Law, true doers and hypocritical doers. The true doers of the Law are those who are moved by faith in Christ to do the Law. The hypocritical doers of the Law are those who seek to obtain righteousness by a mechanical performance of good works while their hearts are far removed from God. They act like the foolish carpenter who starts with the roof when he builds a house. Instead of doing the Law, these law-conscious hypocrites break the Law. They break the very first commandment of God by denying His promise in Christ. They do not worship God in faith. They worship themselves.

Those who intend to obtain righteousness by their own efforts do not say in so many words: "I am God; I am Christ." But it amounts to that. They usurp the divinity and office of Christ. The effect is the same as if they said, "I am Christ; I am a Savior. I save myself and others."

Indeed, works do follow after faith, but faith is not therefore a meritorious work. Faith is a gift. The character and limitations of the Law must be rigidly maintained.

When we believe in Christ we live by faith. When we believe in the Law we may be active enough but we have no life. The function of the Law is not to give life; the function of the Law is to kill. True, the Law says: "The man that doeth them shall live in them." But where is the person who can do "them," i.e., love God with all his heart, soul, and mind, and his neighbor as himself?

Paul has nothing against those who are justified by faith and therefore are true doers of the Law. He opposes those who think they can fulfill the Law when in reality they can only sin against the Law by trying to obtain righteousness by the Law.

Whatever sins I, you, all of us
have committed or shall commit,
they are Christ's sins
as if He had committed them Himself.

The Accent of 'For Us'

Paul does not say that Christ was made a curse for Himself. The accent is on the two words "for us." Christ is personally innocent. Personally, He did not deserve to be hanged for any crime of His own doing. But because Christ took the place of others who were sinners, He was hanged like any other transgressor. The Law of Moses leaves no loopholes. It says that a transgressor should be hanged. Who are the other sinners? We are. The sentence of death and everlasting damnation had long been pronounced over us. But Christ took all our sins and died for them on the Cross. "He was numbered with the transgressors; and he bare the sin of many, and made intercession for the transgressors." (Isaiah 53:12.)

All the prophets of old said that Christ should be the greatest transgressor, murderer, adulterer, thief, blasphemer that ever was or ever could be on earth. When He took the sins of the whole world upon Himself, Christ was no longer an innocent person. He was a sinner burdened with the sins of a Paul who was a blasphemer; burdened with the sins of a Peter who denied Christ; burdened with the sins of a David who committed adultery and murder, and gave the heathen occasion to laugh at the Lord. In short, Christ was charged with the sins of all men, that He should pay for them with His own blood. The curse struck Him. The Law found Him among sinners. He was not only in the company of sinners. He had gone so far as to invest Himself with the flesh and blood of sinners. So the Law judged and hanged Him for a sinner.

I am told that it is preposterous and wicked to call the Son of God a cursed sinner. I answer: If you deny that He is a condemned sinner, you are forced to deny that Christ died. It is not less preposterous to say, the Son of God died, than to say, the Son of God was a sinner.

Whatever sins I, you, all of us have committed or shall commit, they are Christ's sins as if He had committed them Himself. Our sins have to be Christ's sins or we shall perish forever.

If Christ bears our sins, we do not bear them. But if Christ is innocent of our sins and does not bear them, we must bear them, and we shall die in our sins. "But thanks be to God, which giveth us the victory through our Lord Jesus Christ." When we hear that Christ was made a curse for us, let us believe it with joy and assurance. By faith Christ changes places with us. He gets our sins, we get His holiness.

To give a human example, brothers: even with a man-made covenant, no one annuls it or adds to it once it has been ratified. Now the promises were made to Abraham and to his offspring. It does not say, "And to offsprings," referring to many, but referring to one, "And to your offspring," who is Christ. This is what I mean: the law, which came 430 years afterward, does not annul a covenant previously ratified by God, so as to make the promise void. For if the inheritance comes by the law, it no longer comes by promise; but God gave it to Abraham by a promise.

Why then the law? It was added because of transgressions, until the offspring should come to whom the promise had been made, and it was put in place through angels by an intermediary. Now an intermediary implies more than one, but God is one.

Is the law then contrary to the promises of God? Certainly not! For if a law had been given that could give life, then righteousness would indeed be by the law. But the Scripture imprisoned everything under sin, so that the promise by faith in Jesus Christ might be given to those who believe. - Galatians 3:15- 22 (ESV)

The question naturally arises: If the Law was not given for righteousness or salvation, why was it given? Why did God give the Law in the first place if it cannot justify a person?

The Jews believed if they kept the Law they would be saved. When they heard that the Gospel proclaimed a Christ who had come into the world to save sinners and not the righteous; when they heard that sinners were to enter the kingdom of heaven before the righteous, the Jews were very much put out. They murmured: "These last have wrought but one hour, and thou hast made them equal unto us, which have borne the burden and heat of the day." (Matthew 20:12.) They complained that the heathen who at one time had been worshipers of idols obtained grace without the drudgery of the Law that was theirs.

42

Today we hear the same complaints. "What was the use of our having lived in a cloister, twenty, thirty, forty years; what was the sense of having vowed chastity, poverty, obedience; what good are all the masses and canonical hours that we read; what profit is there in fasting, praying, etc., if any man or woman, any beggar or scour woman is to be made equal to us, or even be considered more acceptable unto God than we?"

The Twofold Purpose of the Law

The Law has a twofold purpose. One purpose is civil. God has ordained civil laws to punish crime. Every law is given to restrain sin. Does it not then make men righteous? No. In refraining from murder, adultery, theft, or other sins, I do so under compulsion because I fear the jail, the noose, the electric chair. These restrain me as iron bars restrain a lion and a bear. Otherwise they would tear everything to pieces. Such forceful restraint cannot be regarded as righteousness, rather as an indication of unrighteousness. As a wild beast is tied to keep it from running amuck, so the Law bridles mad and furious man to keep him from running wild. The need for restraint shows plainly enough that those who need the Law are not righteous, but wicked men who are fit to be tied. No, the Law does not justify.

The first purpose of the Law, accordingly, is to restrain the wicked. The devil gets people into all kinds of scrapes. Therefore God instituted governments, parents, laws, restrictions, and civil ordinances. At least they help to tie the devil's hands so that he does not rage up and down the earth. This civil restraint by the Law is intended by God for the preservation of all things, particularly for the good of the Gospel that it should not be hindered too much by the tumult of the wicked. But Paul is not now treating of this civil use and function of the Law.

The second purpose of the Law is spiritual and divine. Paul describes this spiritual purpose of the Law in the words, "Because of transgressions," i.e., to reveal to a person his sin, blindness, misery, his ignorance, hatred, and contempt of God, his death, hell, and condemnation.

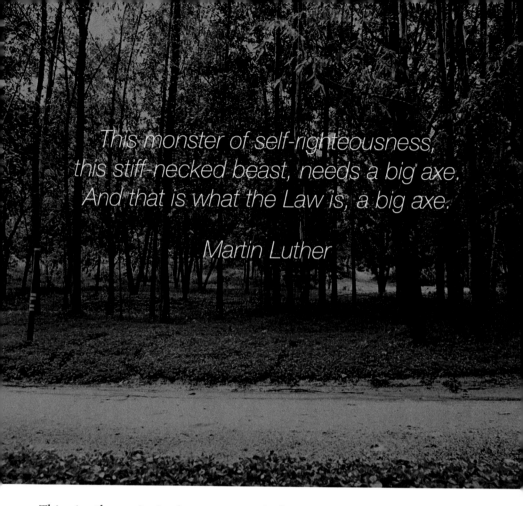

> *This monster of self-righteousness,*
> *this stiff-necked beast, needs a big axe.*
> *And that is what the Law is, a big axe.*
>
> *Martin Luther*

This is the principal purpose of the Law and its most valuable contribution. As long as a person is not a murderer, adulterer, thief, he would swear that he is righteous. How is God going to humble such a person except by the Law? The Law is the hammer of death, the thunder of hell, and the lightning of God's wrath to bring down the proud and shameless hypocrites. When the Law was instituted on Mount Sinai it was accompanied by lightning, by storms, by the sound of trumpets, to tear to pieces that monster called self-righteousness. As long as a person thinks he is right he is going to be incomprehensibly proud and presumptuous. He is going to hate God, despise His grace and mercy, and ignore the promises in Christ. The Gospel of the free forgiveness of sins through Christ will never appeal to the self-righteous.

This monster of self-righteousness, this stiff-necked beast, needs a big axe. And that is what the Law is, a big axe. Accordingly, the proper use and function of the Law is to threaten until the conscience is scared stiff.

The awful spectacle at Mount Sinai portrayed the proper use of the Law. When the children of Israel came out of Egypt a feeling of singular holiness possessed them. They boasted: "We are the people of God. All that the Lord hath spoken we will do." (Ex. 19:8) This feeling of holiness was heightened when Moses ordered them to wash their clothes, to refrain from their wives, and to prepare themselves all around. The third day came and Moses led the people out of their tents to the foot of the mountain into the presence of the Lord. What happened? When the children of Israel saw the whole mountain burning and smoking, the black clouds rent by fierce lightning flashing up and down in the inky darkness, when they heard the sound of the trumpet blowing louder and longer, shattered by the roll of thunder, they were so frightened that they begged Moses: "Speak thou with us, and we will hear: but let not God speak with us, lest we die." (Ex. 20:19.) I ask you, what good did their scrubbing, their snow-white clothes, and their continence do them? No good at all. Not a single one could stand in the presence of the glorious Lord. Stricken by the terror of God, they fled back into their tents, as if the devil were after them.

The Law is meant to produce the same effect today which it produced at Mount Sinai long ago. I want to encourage all who fear God, especially those who intend to become ministers of the Gospel, to learn from the Apostle the proper use of the Law. I fear that after our time the right handling of the Law will become a lost art. Even now, although we continually explain the separate functions of the Law and the Gospel, we have those among us who do not understand how the Law should be used. What will it be like when we are dead and gone?

We want it understood that we do not reject the Law as our opponents claim. On the contrary, we uphold the Law. We say the Law is good if it is used for the purposes for which it was designed, to check civil transgression, and to magnify spiritual transgressions. The Law is also a light like the Gospel. But instead of revealing the grace of God, righteousness, and life, the Law brings sin, death, and the wrath of God to light. This is the business of the Law, and here the business of the Law ends, and should go no further.

The business of the Gospel, on the other hand, is to quicken, to comfort, to raise the fallen. The Gospel carries the news that God for Christ's sake is merciful to the most unworthy sinners, if they will only believe that Christ by His death has delivered them from sin and everlasting death unto grace, forgiveness, and everlasting life. By keeping in mind the difference between the Law and the Gospel we let each perform its special task. Of this difference between the Law and the Gospel nothing can be discovered in the writings of the monks or scholastics, nor for that matter in the writings of the ancient fathers. Augustine understood the difference somewhat. Jerome and others knew nothing of it. The silence in the Church concerning the difference between the Law and the Gospel has resulted in untold harm. Unless a sharp distinction is maintained between the purpose and function of the Law and the Gospel, the Christian doctrine cannot be kept free from error.

Look in the Mirror

The Law is a mirror to show a person what he is like, a sinner who is guilty of death, and worthy of everlasting punishment. What is this bruising and beating by the hand of the Law to accomplish? This, that we may find the way to grace. The Law is an usher to lead the way to grace. God is the God of the humble, the miserable, the afflicted. It is His nature to exalt the humble, to comfort the sorrowing, to heal the broken-hearted, to justify the sinners, and to save the condemned. The fatuous idea that a person can be holy by himself denies God the pleasure of saving sinners. God must therefore first take the sledge-hammer of the Law in His fists and smash the beast of self-righteousness and its brood of self-confidence, self-wisdom, self-righteousness, and self-help. When the conscience has been thoroughly frightened by the Law it welcomes the Gospel of grace with its message of a Savior who came into the world, not to break the bruised reed, nor to quench the smoking flax, but to preach glad tidings to the poor, to heal the broken-hearted, and to grant forgiveness of sins to all the captives.

God must therefore first take
the sledge-hammer of the Law
in His fists and smash the beast of self-righteousness
and its brood of self-confidence, self-wisdom,
self-righteousness, and self-help.

Man's folly, however, is so prodigious that instead of embracing the message of grace with its guarantee of the forgiveness of sin for Christ's sake, man finds himself more laws to satisfy his conscience. "If I live," says he, "I will mend my life. I will do this, I will do that."

When the Law drives you to the point of despair, let it drive you a little farther, let it drive you straight into the arms of Jesus who says: "Come unto me, all ye that labour and are heavy laden, and I will give you rest."

In Christian theology the Law does not justify. In fact it has the contrary effect. The Law alarms us, it magnifies our sins until we begin to hate the Law and its divine Author. Would you call this being justified by the Law?

The Law can do nothing for us except to arouse the conscience. Before the Law comes to me I feel no sin. But when the Law comes, sin, death, and hell are revealed to me. You would not call this being made righteous. You would call it being condemned to death and hell-fire.

Before he digressed Paul stated that the Law does not justify.

Shall we then discard the Law? No, no. It supplies a certain need. It supplies men with a needed realization of their sinfulness. Now arises another question: If the Law does no more than to reveal sin, does it not oppose the promises of God? The Jews believed that by the restraint and discipline of the Law the promises of God would be hastened, in fact earned by them.

Paul answers: "Not so. On the contrary, if we pay too much attention to the Law the promises of God will be slowed up. How can God fulfill His promises to a people that hates the Law?"

The Law cannot give life. It kills. The Law does not justify a person before God; it increases sin. The Law does not secure righteousness; it hinders righteousness. The Apostle declares emphatically that the Law of itself cannot save.

Despite the intelligibility of Paul's statement, our enemies fail to grasp it. Otherwise they would not emphasize free will, natural strength, the works of supererogation, etc. To escape the charge of forgery they always have their convenient annotation handy, that Paul is referring only to the ceremonial and not to the moral law. But Paul includes all laws.."

There is no law by which righteousness may be obtained, not a single one. God saw that the universal illusion of self-righteousness could not be put down in any other way but by the Law. The Law dispels all self-illusions. It puts the fear of God in a man. Without this fear there can be no thirst for God's mercy. God accordingly uses the Law for a hammer to break up the illusion of self-righteousness, that we should despair of our own strength and efforts at self-justification.

> *Now before faith came, we were held captive under the law, imprisoned until the coming faith would be revealed. So then, the law was our guardian until Christ came, in order that we might be justified by faith. But now that faith has come, we are no longer under a guardian, for in Christ Jesus you are all sons of God, through faith. For as many of you as were baptized into Christ have put on Christ. There is neither Jew nor Greek, there is neither slave nor free, there is no male and female, for you are all one in Christ Jesus. And if you are Christ's, then you are Abraham's offspring, heirs according to promise. - Galatians 3:23-29 (ESV)*

The Law is a prison to those who have not as yet obtained grace. No prisoner enjoys the confinement. He hates it. If he could he would smash the prison and find his freedom at all cost. As long as he stays in prison he refrains from evil deeds. Not because he wants to, but because he has to. The bars and the chains restrain him. He does not regret the crime that put him in jail. On the contrary, he is mighty sore that he cannot rob and kill as before. If he could escape he would go right back to robbing and killing.

The Law enforces good behavior, at least outwardly. We obey the Law because if we don't we will be punished. Our obedience is inspired by fear. We obey under duress and we do it resentfully. Now what kind of righteousness is this when we refrain from evil out of fear of punishment? Hence, the righteousness of the Law is at bottom nothing but love of sin and hatred of righteousness.

All the same, the Law accomplishes this much, that it will outwardly at least and to a certain extent repress vice and crime.

But the Law is also a spiritual prison, a veritable hell. When the Law begins to threaten a person with death and the eternal wrath of God, a man just cannot find any comfort at all. He cannot shake off at will the nightmare of terror which the Law stirs up in his conscience. Of this terror of the Law the Psalms furnish many glimpses.

The Law is a civil and a spiritual prison. And such it should be. For that the Law is intended. Only the confinement in the prison of the Law must not be unduly prolonged. It must come to an end. The freedom of faith must succeed the imprisonment of the Law.

Accordingly each Christian continues to experience in his heart times of the Law and times of the Gospel. The times of the Law are discernible by heaviness of heart, by a lively sense of sin, and a feeling of despair brought on by the Law. These periods of the Law will come again and again as long as we live. To mention my own case. There are many times when I find fault with God and am impatient with Him. The wrath and the judgment of God displease me, my wrath and impatience displease Him. Then is the season of the Law, when "the flesh lusteth against the Spirit, and the Spirit against the flesh."

The time of grace returns when the heart is enlivened by the promise of God's mercy. It soliloquizes: "Why art thou cast down, O my soul? and why art thou disquieted within me? Can you see nothing but law, sin, death, and hell? Is there no grace, no forgiveness, no joy, peace, life, heaven, no Christ and God? Trouble me no more, my soul. Hope in God who has not spared His own dear Son but has given Him into death for thy sins." When the Law carries things too far, say: "Mister Law, you are not the whole show. There are other and better things than you. They tell me to trust in the Lord."

There is a time for the Law and a time for grace. Let us study to be good timekeepers. It is not easy. Law and grace may be miles apart in essence, but in the heart, they are pretty close together. In the heart fear and trust, sin and grace, Law and Gospel cross paths continually.

There is a time for the Law and a time for grace.
Let us study to be good timekeepers.

Whether reason hears that justification before God is obtained by grace alone, it draws the inference that the Law is without value. The doctrine of the Law must therefore be studied carefully lest we either reject the Law altogether, or are tempted to attribute to the Law a capacity to save.

The Apostle declares that we are free from the Law. Christ fulfilled the Law for us. We may live in joy and safety under Christ. The trouble is, our flesh will not let us believe in Christ with all our heart. The fault lies not with Christ, but with us. Sin clings to us as long as we live and spoils our happiness in Christ. Hence, we are only partly free from the Law. "With the mind I myself serve the law of God; but with the flesh the law of sin." (Romans 7:25.)

As far as the conscience is concerned it may cheerfully ignore the Law. But because sin continues to dwell in the flesh, the Law waits around to molest our conscience. More and more, however, Christ increases our faith and in the measure in which our faith is increased, sin, Law, and flesh subside.

If anybody objects to the Gospel and the sacraments on the ground that Christ has taken away our sins once and for always, you will know what to answer. You will answer: Indeed, Christ has taken away my sins. But my flesh, the world, and the devil interfere with my faith. The little light of faith in my heart does not shine all over me at once. It is a gradual diffusion. In the meanwhile I console myself with the thought that eventually my flesh will be made perfect in the resurrection.

Clothed with Christ
To put on Christ according to the Gospel means to clothe oneself with the righteousness, wisdom, power, life, and Spirit of Christ. By nature

we are clad in the garb of Adam. This garb Paul likes to call "the old man." Before we can become the children of God this old man must be put off, as Paul says, Ephesians 4:29. The garment of Adam must come off like soiled clothes. Of course, it is not as simple as changing one's clothes. But God makes it simple. He clothes us with the righteousness of Christ by means of Baptism, as the Apostle says in this verse: "As many of you as have been baptized into Christ have put on Christ." With this change of garments a new birth, a new life stirs in us. New affections toward God spring up in the heart. New determinations affect our will. All this is to put on Christ according to the Gospel. Needless to say, when we have put on the robe of the righteousness of Christ we must not forget to put on also the mantle of the imitation of Christ.

With this statement Paul deals a death blow to the Law. When a person has put on Christ nothing else matters. Whether a person is a Jew, a punctilious and circumcised observer of the Law of Moses, or whether a person is a noble and wise Greek does not matter. Circumstances, personal worth, character, achievements have no bearing upon justification. Before God they count for nothing. What counts is that we put on Christ.

Whether a servant performs his duties well; whether those who are in authority govern wisely; whether a man marries, provides for his family, and is an honest citizen; whether a woman is chaste, obedient to her husband, and a good mother: all these advantages do not qualify a person for salvation. These virtues are commendable, of course; but they do not count points for justification. All the best laws, ceremonies, religions, and deeds of the world cannot take away sin guilt, cannot dispatch death, cannot purchase life.

There is much disparity among men in the world, but there is no such disparity before God. "For all have sinned, and come short of the glory of God." (Romans 3:23.) Let the Jews, let the Greeks, let the whole world keep silent in the presence of God. Those who are justified are justified by Christ. Without faith in Christ the Jew with his laws, the monk with his holy orders, the Greek with his wisdom, the servant with his obedience, shall perish forever.

There is much imparity among men in the world. And it is a good thing. If the woman would change places with the man, if the son would change places with the father, the servant with the master, nothing but confusion would result. In Christ, however, all are equal. We all have one and the same Gospel, "one faith, one baptism, one God and Father of all," one Christ and Savior of all. The Christ of Peter, Paul, and all the saints is our Christ. Paul can always be depended on to add the conditional clause, "In Christ Jesus." If we lose sight of Christ, we lose out.

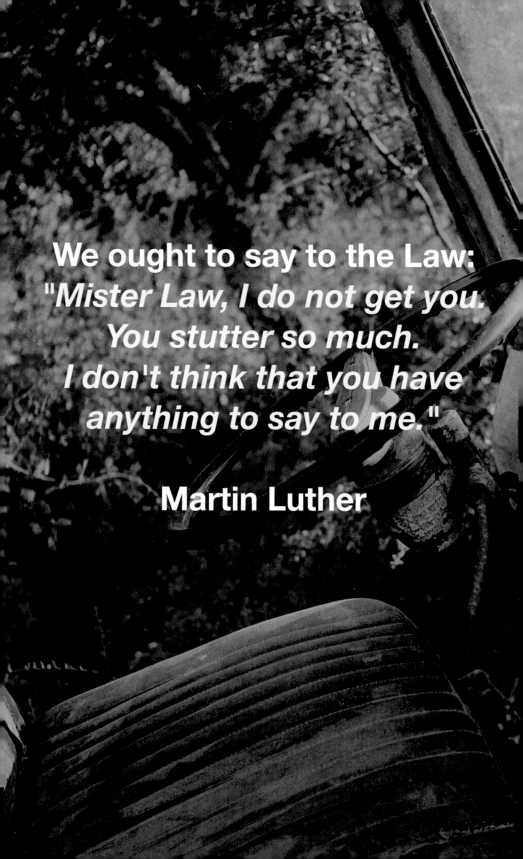

We ought to say to the Law:
"Mister Law, I do not get you.
You stutter so much.
I don't think that you have
anything to say to me."

Martin Luther

Slaves to Sons
Chapter 4

> *What I am saying is that as long as an heir is underage, he is no different from a slave, although he owns the whole estate. The heir is subject to guardians and trustees until the time set by his father. So also, when we were underage, we were in slavery under the elemental spiritual forces of the world. But when the set time had fully come, God sent his Son, born of a woman, born under the law, to redeem those under the law, that we might receive adoption to sonship. Because you are his sons, God sent the Spirit of his Son into our hearts, the Spirit who calls out, "Abba, Father." So you are no longer a slave, but God's child; and since you are his child, God has made you also an heir.* - Galatians 4:1-7 (NIV)

I do not mean to give the impression that the Law should be despised. Neither does Paul intend to leave that impression. The Law ought to be honored.

But when it is a matter of justification before God, Paul had to speak disparagingly of the Law, because the Law has nothing to do with justification. If it thrusts its nose into the business of justification we must talk harshly to the Law to keep it in its place. The conscience ought not to be on speaking terms with the Law. The conscience ought to know only Christ. To say this is easy, but in times of trial, when the conscience writhes in the presence of God, it is not so easy to do. As such times we are to believe in Christ as if there were no Law or sin anywhere, but only Christ. We ought to say to the Law: "Mister Law, I do not get you. You stutter so much. I don't think that you have anything to say to me."

When it is not a question of salvation or justification with us, we are to think highly of the Law and call it "holy, just, and good." (Romans 7:12) The Law is of no comfort to a stricken conscience. Therefore it should not be allowed to rule in our conscience, particularly in view of the fact that Christ paid so great a price to deliver the conscience from the tyranny of the Law. Let us understand that the Law and Christ are impossible bedfellows.

The Work of the Spirit

This renewal by the Holy Spirit may not be conspicuous to the world, but it is patent to us by our better judgment, our improved speech, and our unashamed confession of Christ. Formerly we did not confess Christ to be our only merit, as we do now in the light of the Gospel. Why, then, should we feel bad if the world looks upon us as ravagers of religion and insurgents against constituted authority? We confess Christ and our conscience approves of it. Then, too, we live in the fear of God. If we sin, we sin not on purpose, but unwittingly, and we are sorry for it. Sin sticks in our flesh, and the flesh gets us into sin even after we have been imbued by the Holy Ghost. Outwardly there is no great difference between a Christian and any honest man. The activities of a Christian are not sensational. He performs his duty according to his vocation. He takes good care of his family, and is kind and helpful to others. Such homely, everyday performances are not much admired. But the setting-up exercises of the monks draw great applause. Holy works, you know. Only the acts of a Christian are truly good and acceptable to God, because they are done in faith, with a cheerful heart, out of gratitude to Christ.

We ought to have no misgivings about whether the Holy Ghost dwells in us. We are "the temple of the Holy Ghost." (I Cor. 3:16.) When we have a love for the Word of God, and gladly hear, talk, write, and think of Christ, we are to know that this inclination toward Christ is the gift and work of the Holy Ghost. Where you come across contempt for the Word of God, there is the devil. We meet with such contempt for the Word of God mostly among the common people. They act as though the Word of God does not concern them. Wherever you find a love for the Word, thank God for the Holy Spirit who infuses this love into the hearts of men. We never come by this love naturally, neither can it be enforced by laws. It is the gift of the Holy Spirit.

We ought to feel sure that we stand in the grace of God, not in view of our own worthiness, but through the good services of Christ.

As certain as we are that Christ pleases God, so sure ought we to be that we also please God, because Christ is in us. And although we daily offend God by our sins, yet as often as we sin, God's mercy bends over us. Therefore sin cannot get us to doubt the grace of God. Our certainty is of Christ, that mighty Hero who overcame the Law, sin, death, and all evils. So long as He sits at the right hand of God to intercede for us, we have nothing to fear from the anger of God.

> We ought to feel sure that we stand in the grace of God, not in view of our own worthiness, but through the good services of Christ.

If we could be fully persuaded that we are in the good grace of God, that our sins are forgiven, that we have the Spirit of Christ, that we are the beloved children of God, we would be ever so happy and grateful to God. But because we often feel fear and doubt we cannot come to that happy certainty.

Train your conscience to believe that God approves of you. Fight it out with doubt. Gain assurance through the Word of God. Say: "I am all right with God. I have the Holy Ghost. Christ, in whom I do believe, makes me worthy. I gladly hear, read, sing, and write of Him. I would like nothing better than that Christ's Gospel be known throughout the world and that many, many be brought to faith in Him."

Let us not fail to thank God for delivering us from the doctrine of doubt. The Gospel commands us to look away from our own good works to the promises of God in Christ, the Mediator. The pope commands us to look away from the promises of God in Christ to our own merit. No wonder they are the eternal prey of doubt and despair. We depend upon God for salvation. No wonder that our doctrine is certified, because it does not rest in our own strength, our own conscience, our own feelings, our own person, our own works. It is built on a better foundation. It is built on the promises and truth of God.

Let us never doubt the mercy of God in Christ Jesus, but make up our minds that God is pleased with us, that He looks after us, and that we have the Holy Spirit who prays for us.

From Slaves to Sons

What ever induced God to adopt us for His children and heirs?

What claim can men who are subservient to sin, subject to the curse of the Law, and worthy of everlasting death, have on God and eternal life? That God adopted us is due to the merit of Jesus Christ, the Son of God, who humbled Himself under the Law and redeemed us law-ridden sinners.

Paul says: "With the Holy Spirit in our hearts crying, 'Abba, Father,' there can be no doubt that God has adopted us for His children and that our subjection to the Law has come to an end." We are now the free children of God. We may now say to the Law: "Mister Law, you have lost your throne to Christ. I am free now and a son of God. You cannot curse me any more." Do not permit the Law to lie in your conscience. Your conscience belongs to Christ. Let Christ be in it and not the Law.

As the children of God we are the heirs of His eternal heaven. What a wonderful gift heaven is, man's heart cannot conceive, much less describe. Until we enter upon our heavenly inheritance we are only to have our little faith to go by. To man's reason our faith looks rather forlorn. But because our faith rests on the promises of the infinite God, His promises are also infinite, so much so that nothing can accuse or condemn us.

A son is an heir, not by virtue of high accomplishments, but by virtue of his birth. He is a mere recipient. His birth makes him an heir, not his labors. In exactly the same way we obtain the eternal gifts of righteousness, resurrection, and everlasting life. We obtain them not as agents, but as beneficiaries. We are the children and heirs of God through faith in Christ. We have Christ to thank for everything.

We are not the heirs of some rich and mighty man, but heirs of God, the almighty Creator of all things. If a person could fully appreciate what it means to be a son and heir of God, he would rate the might and wealth of nations small change in comparison with his heavenly inheritance. What is the world to him who has heaven?

But the law of the members strives against the law of the mind, and makes perfect joy and faith impossible. We need the continued help and comfort of the Holy Spirit. We need His prayers. Paul himself cried out: "O wretched man that I am! Who shall deliver me from the body of this death?" The body of this death spoiled the joy of his spirit. He did not always entertain the sweet and glad expectation of his heavenly inheritance. He often felt miserable.

This goes to show how hard it is to believe. Faith is feeble, because the flesh wars against the spirit. If we could have perfect faith, our loathing for this life in the world would be complete. We would not be so careful about this life. We would not be so attached to the world and the things of the world. We would not feel so good when we have them; we would not feel so bad when we lose them. We would be far more humble and patient and kind. But our faith is weak, because our spirit is weak. In this life we can have only the first-fruits of the Spirit, as Paul says.

The Apostle always has Christ on the tip of his tongue.

Therefore he talks of Christ continually. As often as he speaks of righteousness, grace, the promise, the adoption, and the inheritance of heaven, he adds the words, "In Christ," or "Through Christ," to show that these blessings are not to be had by the Law, or the deeds of the Law, much less by our own exertions, or by the observance of human traditions, but only by and through and in Christ.

Formerly, when you did not know God, you were slaves to those who by nature are not gods. But now that you know God—or rather are known by God—how is it that you are turning back to those weak and miserable forces? Do you wish to be enslaved by them all over again? You are observing special days and months and seasons and years! I fear for you, that somehow I have wasted my efforts on you. - Galatians 4:8-11 (NIV)

This concludes Paul's discourse on justification. From now to the end of the Epistle the Apostle writes mostly of Christian conduct. But before he follows up his doctrinal discourse with practical precepts he once more reproves the Galatians.

He is deeply displeased with them for relinquishing their divine doctrine. He tells them: "You have taken on teachers who intend to recommit you to the Law. By my doctrine I called you out of the darkness of ignorance into the wonderful light of the knowledge of God. I led you out of bondage into the freedom of the sons of God, not by the prescription of laws, but by the gift of heavenly and eternal blessings through Christ Jesus. How could you so soon forsake the light and return to darkness? How could you so quickly stray from grace into the Law, from freedom into bondage?"

We are careful to apply the Gospel and the Law in their proper turn. Yet we make little headway because the devil seduces people into misbelief by taking Christ out of their sight and focusing their eyes upon the Law.

Paul seems to identify their defection from the Gospel to the Law with their former idolatry. Indeed he does. Whoever gives up the article of justification does not know the true God. It is one and the same thing whether a person reverts to the Law or to the worship of idols. When the article of justification is lost, nothing remains except error, hypocrisy, godlessness, and idolatry.

Without the doctrine of justification there can be only ignorance of God. Those who refuse to be justified by Christ are idolaters. They remain under the Law, sin, death, and the power of the devil. Everything they do is wrong.

Nowadays there are many such idolaters who want to be counted among the true confessors of the Gospel. They may even teach that men are delivered from their sins by the death of Christ. But because they attach more importance to charity than to faith in Christ they dishonor Him and pervert His Word. They do not serve the true God, but an idol of their own invention. The true God has never yet smiled upon a person for his charity or virtues, but only for the sake of Christ's merits.

The objection is frequently raised that the Bible commands that we should love God with all our heart. True enough. But because God commands it, it does not follow that we do it. If we could love God with all our heart we should undoubtedly be justified by our obedience, for it is written, "Which if a man do, he shall live in them." (Lev. 18:5.) But now comes the Gospel and says: "Because you do not do these things, you cannot live in them." The words, "Thou shalt love the Lord, thy God," require perfect obedience, perfect fear, perfect trust, and perfect love. But where are the people who can render perfection? Hence, this commandment, instead of justifying men, only accuses and condemns them. "Christ is the end of the law for righteousness to every one that believeth" (Romans 10:1.)

If you care to amplify this matter you may add the observation that the Law is a weak and beggarly element because it makes people weak and beggarly. The Law has no power and affluence to make men strong and rich before God. To seek to be justified by the Law amounts to the same thing as if a person who is already weak and feeble should try to find strength in weakness, or as if a person with the dropsy should seek a cure by exposing himself to the pestilence, or as if a leper should go to a leper, and a beggar to a beggar to find health and wealth.

Those who seek to be justified by the Law grow weaker and more destitute right along. They are weak and bankrupt to begin with. They are by nature the children of wrath. Yet for salvation they grasp at the straw of the Law. The Law can only aggravate their weakness and poverty. The Law makes them ten times weaker and poorer than they were before.

I and many others have experienced the truth of this. I have known monks who zealously labored to please God for salvation, but the more they labored the more impatient, miserable, uncertain, and fearful they became. What else can you expect? You cannot grow strong through weakness and rich through poverty. People who prefer the Law to the Gospel are like Aesop's dog who let go of the meat to snatch at the shadow of the water. There is no satisfaction in the Law. What satisfaction can there be in collecting laws with which to torment oneself and others? One law breeds ten more until their number is legion.

I plead with you, brothers and sisters, become like me, for I became like you. You did me no wrong. As you know, it was because of an illness that I first preached the gospel to you, and even though my illness was a trial to you, you did not treat me with contempt or scorn. Instead, you welcomed me as if I were an angel of God, as if I were Christ Jesus himself. Where, then, is your blessing of me now? I can testify that, if you could have done so, you would have torn out your eyes and given them to me. Have I now become your enemy by telling you the truth?

Those people are zealous to win you over, but for no good. What they want is to alienate you from us, so that you may have zeal for them. It is fine to be zealous, provided the purpose is good, and to be so always, not just when I am with you. My dear children, for whom I am again in the pains of childbirth until Christ is formed in you, how I wish I could be with you now and change my tone, because I am perplexed about you! - Galatians 4:12-20 (NIV)

Paul's reason for praising the Galatians is to avoid giving them the impression as if he were their enemy because he had reprimanded them.

A true friend will admonish his erring brother, and if the erring brother has any sense at all he will thank his friend. In the world truth produces hatred. Whoever speaks the truth is counted an enemy. But among friends it is not so, much less among Christians. The Apostle wants his Galatians to know that just because he had told them the truth they are not to think that he dislikes them. "I told you the truth because I love you."

Paul was considerably disturbed by the commissions and changes that followed in the wake of his preaching. He was accused of being "a pestilent fellow, a mover of sedition among all the Jews throughout the world." (Acts 24:5.) In Philippi the townspeople cried that he troubled their city and taught customs which were not lawful for them to receive. (Acts 16:20, 21.)

All troubles, calamities, famines, wars were laid to the charge of the Gospel of the apostles.

Do you think for a moment that these reactions did not worry the apostles? They were not made of iron. They foresaw the revolutionary character of the Gospel. They also foresaw the dissensions that would creep into the Church. It was bad news for Paul when he heard that the Corinthians were denying the resurrection of the dead, that the churches he had planted were experiencing all kinds of difficulties, and that the Gospel was being supplanted by false doctrines.

But Paul also knew that the Gospel was not to blame. He did not resign his office because he knew that the Gospel he preached was the power of God unto salvation to every one that believes.

The same criticism which was leveled at the apostles is leveled at us. All of these vilifications cannot discourage us. We know that there is nothing the devil hates worse than the Gospel.

*We know that there is nothing
the devil hates worse than the Gospel.*

Here Paul would have closed his Epistle because he did not know what else to say. He wishes he could see the Galatians in person and straighten out their difficulties. But he is not sure whether the Galatians have fully understood the difference between the Gospel and the Law. To make sure, he introduces another illustration.

He knows people like illustrations and stories. He knows that Christ Himself made ample use of parables.

Tell me, you who want to be under the law, are you not aware of what the law says? For it is written that Abraham had two sons, one by the slave woman and the other by the free woman. His son by the slave woman was born according to the flesh, but his son by the free woman was born as the result of a divine promise.

These things are being taken figuratively: The women represent two covenants. One covenant is from Mount Sinai and bears children who are to be slaves: This is Hagar. Now Hagar stands for Mount Sinai in Arabia and corresponds to the present city of Jerusalem, because she is in slavery with her children. But the Jerusalem that is above is free, and she is our mother. For it is written:

"Be glad, barren woman,
    you who never bore a child;
shout for joy and cry aloud,
    you who were never in labor;
because more are the children of the desolate woman
    than of her who has a husband."

Now you, brothers and sisters, like Isaac, are children of promise. At that time the son born according to the flesh persecuted the son born by the power of the Spirit. It is the same now. But what does Scripture say? "Get rid of the slave woman and her son, for the slave woman's son will never share in the inheritance with the free woman's son." Therefore, brothers and sisters, we are not children of the slave woman, but of the free woman. - Galatians 4:21-30 (NIV)

The allegory which Paul is about to bring is taken from the Book of Genesis.

Abraham had two sons: Ishmael by Hagar, and Isaac by Sarah. They were both the true sons of Abraham, with this difference, that Ishmael was born after the flesh, i.e., without the commandment and promise of God, while Isaac was born according to the promise.

With the permission of Sarah, Abraham took Hagar, Sarah's bondwoman, to wife. Sarah knew that God had promised to make her husband Abraham the father of a nation, and she hoped that she would be the mother of this promised nation. But with the passage of the years her hope died out. In order that the promise of God should not be annulled by her barrenness this holy woman resigned her right and honor to her maid. This was no easy thing for her to do. She abased herself. She thought: "God is no liar. What He has promised He will perform. But perhaps God does not want me to be the mother of Abraham's posterity. Perhaps He prefers Hagar for the honor."

Ishmael was thus born without a special word or promise of God, at the mere request of Sarah. God did not command Abraham to take Hagar, nor did God promise to bless the coalition. It is evident that Ishmael was the son of Abraham after the flesh, and not after the promise.

In the ninth chapter of the Epistle to the Romans St. Paul advances the same argument which he amplifies into an allegory in writing to the Galatians. There he argues that all the children of Abraham are not the children of God. For Abraham had two kinds of children, children born of the promise, like Isaac, and other children born without the promise, as Ishmael. With this argument Paul squelched the proud Jews who gloried that they were the children of God because they were the seed and the children of Abraham. Paul makes it clear enough that it takes more than an Abrahamic pedigree to be a child of God. To be a child of God requires faith in Christ.

He applies this prophecy to Hagar and Sarah, to the Law and the Gospel.

The Law as the husband of the fruitful woman procreates many children. For men of all ages have had the idea that they are right when they follow after the Law and outwardly perform its requirements.

Although the Law has many children, they are not free. They are slaves. As servants they cannot have a share in the inheritance, but are driven from the house as Ishmael was cast out of the house of Abraham.

On the other hand, Sarah, the free Church, seems barren. The Gospel of the Cross which the Church proclaims does not have the appeal that the Law has for men, and therefore it does not find many adherents. The Church does not look prosperous. Unbelievers have always predicted the death of the Church. The Jews were quite certain that the Church would not long endure. They said to Paul: "As concerning this sect, we know that everywhere it is spoken against." (Acts 28:22.) No matter how barren and forsaken, how weak and desolate the Church may seem, she alone is really fruitful before God. By the Gospel she procreates an infinite number of children that are free heirs of everlasting life.

The Law, "the old husband," is really dead. But not all people know it, or want to know it. They labor and bear the burden and the heat of the day, and bring forth many children, children that are bastards like themselves, children born to be put out of the house like Ishmael to perish forever.

"There is now no condemnation to them which are in Christ Jesus."- Romans 8:1

"If the Son shall make you free, ye shall be free indeed." (John 8:36.)

You will complain: "But I am not doing anything." That is right. You cannot do a thing to be delivered from the tyranny of the Law. But listen to the glad tidings which the Holy Ghost brings to you in the words of

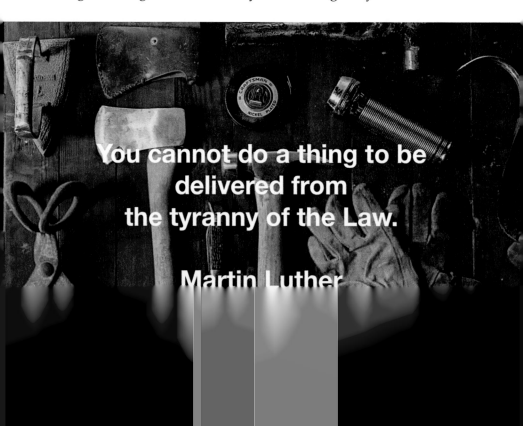

You cannot do a thing to be delivered from the tyranny of the Law.

Martin Luther

the prophet: "Rejoice, thou barren." As Christ is greater than the Law, so much more excellent is the righteousness of Christ than the righteousness of the Law.

This is a cheering thought. We who are born of the Gospel, and live in Christ, and rejoice in our inheritance, have Ishmael for our enemy. The children of the Law will always persecute the children of the Gospel. This is our daily experience. Our opponents tell us that everything was at peace before the Gospel was revived by us. Since then the whole world has been upset. People blame us and the Gospel for everything, for the disobedience of subjects to their rulers, for wars, plagues, and famines, for revolutions, and every other evil that can be imagined.

We invite our opponents to tell us what good things attended the preaching of the Gospel by the apostles. Our opponents blame our doctrine for the present turmoil. But ours is a doctrine of grace and peace. It does not stir up trouble.

At any rate, our opponents cannot accuse us of adultery, murder, theft, and such crimes. The worst they can say about us is that we have the Gospel. What is wrong with the Gospel? We teach that Christ, the Son of God, has redeemed us from sin and everlasting death. This is not our doctrine. It belongs to Christ. If there is anything wrong with it, it is not our fault. If they want to condemn Christ for being our Savior and Redeemer, that is their lookout. We are mere onlookers, watching to see who will win the victory, Christ or His opponents.

On one occasion Jesus remarked: "If ye were of the world, the world would love his own, but because ye are not of the world, but I have chosen you out of the world, therefore the world hateth you." (John 15:19.) In other words: "I am the cause of all your troubles. I am the one for whose sake you are killed. If you did not confess my name, the world would not hate you. The servant is not greater than his lord. If they have persecuted me, they will also persecute you."

Christ takes all the blame. He says: "You have not incurred the hatred and persecutions of the world. I have. But be of good cheer; I have overcome the world."

"So, brothers, we are not children of the slave but of the free woman." -
Galatians 4:31 (ESV)

With this sentence the Apostle Paul concludes his allegory of the barren Church. This sentence forms a clear rejection of the righteousness of the Law and a confirmation of the doctrine of justification. In the next chapter Paul lays special stress upon the freedom which the children of the free woman enjoy.

He treats of Christian liberty, the knowledge of which is very necessary. The liberty which Christ purchased for us is a bulwark to us in our battle against spiritual tyranny. Therefore we must carefully study this doctrine of Christian liberty, not only for the confirmation of the doctrine of justification, but also for the comfort and encouragement of those who are weak in faith.

If we only teach works... we shall lose the faith.
If we only teach faith people will come to think
that good works are superfluous.

Martin Luther

Freedom in Christ
Chapter 5

For freedom Christ has set us free; stand firm therefore, and do not submit again to a yoke of slavery.

Look: I, Paul, say to you that if you accept circumcision, Christ will be of no advantage to you. I testify again to every man who accepts circumcision that he is obligated to keep the whole law. You are severed from Christ, you who would be justified by the law; you have fallen away from grace. For through the Spirit, by faith, we ourselves eagerly wait for the hope of righteousness. For in Christ Jesus neither circumcision nor uncircumcision counts for anything, but only faith working through love. - Galatians 5:1-6 (ESV)

In this chapter the Apostle Paul presents the doctrine of Christian liberty in a final effort to persuade the Galatians to give up the nefarious doctrine of the false apostles. To accomplish his purpose he adduces threats and promises, trying in every way possible to keep them in the liberty which Christ purchased for them.

"Be steadfast, not careless. Lie not down and sleep, but stand up. Be watchful. Hold fast the liberty wherewith Christ hath made you free." Those who loll cannot keep this liberty. Satan hates the light of the Gospel. When it begins to shine a little he fights against it with might and main.

What liberty does Paul mean? Not civil liberty (for which we have the government to thank), but the liberty which Christ has procured for us.

Paul is speaking of a far better liberty, the liberty "wherewith Christ hath made us free," not from material bonds, not from the Babylonian captivity, not from the tyranny of the Turks, but from the eternal wrath of God.

Where is this liberty?

In the conscience.

Our conscience is free and quiet because it no longer has to fear the wrath of God. This is real liberty, compared with which every other kind of liberty is not worth mentioning. Who can adequately express the boon that comes to a person when he has the heart-assurance that God will nevermore be angry with him, but will forever be merciful to him for Christ's sake? This is indeed a marvelous liberty, to have the sovereign God for our Friend and Father who will defend, maintain, and save us in this life and in the life to come.

Our conscience is free and quiet
because it no longer has to fear the wrath of God.

As an outgrowth of this liberty, we are at the same time free from the Law, sin, death, the power of the devil, hell, etc. Since the wrath of God

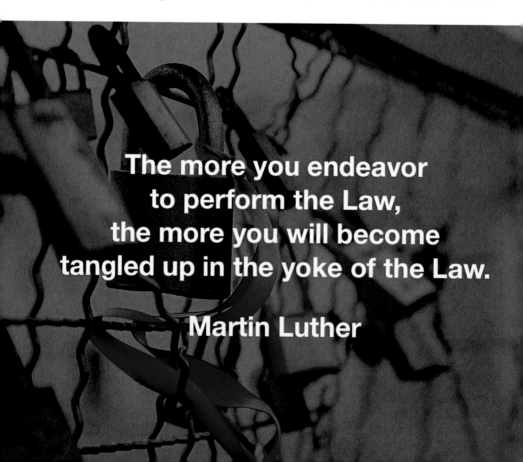

The more you endeavor
to perform the Law,
the more you will become
tangled up in the yoke of the Law.

Martin Luther

has been assuaged by Christ no Law, sin, or death may now accuse and condemn us. These foes of ours will continue to frighten us, but not too much. The worth of our Christian liberty cannot be exaggerated.

Our conscience must be trained to fall back on the freedom purchased for us by Christ. Though the fears of the Law, the terrors of sin, the horror of death assail us occasionally, we know that these feelings shall not endure, because the prophet quotes God as saying: "In a little wrath I hid my face from thee for a moment: but with everlasting kindness will I have mercy on thee." (Isa. 54:8.)

We shall appreciate this liberty all the more when we bear in mind that it was Jesus Christ, the Son of God, who purchased it with His own blood. Hence, Christ's liberty is given us not by the Law, or for our own righteousness, but freely for Christ's sake. In the eighth chapter of the Gospel of St. John, Jesus declares: "If the Son shall make you free, ye shall be free indeed." He only stands between us and the evils which trouble and afflict us and which He has overcome for us.

Our liberty is founded on Christ Himself, who sits at the right hand of God and intercedes for us. Therefore our liberty is sure and valid as long as we believe in Christ. As long as we cling to Him with a steadfast faith we possess His priceless gifts. But if we are careless and indifferent we shall lose them. It is not without good reason that Paul urges us to watch and to stand fast. He knew that the devil delights in taking this liberty away from us.

The Yoke of Bondage

This passage may well serve as a criterion for all the religions. To teach that besides faith in Christ other devices like works, or the observance of rules, traditions, or ceremonies are necessary for the attainment of righteousness and everlasting life, is to make Christ and His salvation of no benefit to anybody.

Let us bear this in mind when the devil accuses our conscience. When that dragon accuses us of having done no good at all, but only evil, say to him: "You trouble me with the remembrance of my past sins; you remind me that I have done no good. But this does not bother me, because if I were to trust in my own good deeds, or despair because I have done no good deeds, Christ would profit me neither way. I am not going to make him unprofitable to me. This I would do, if I should presume to purchase for myself the favor of God and everlasting life by my good deeds, or if I should despair of my salvation because of my sins."

The more you endeavor to perform the Law, the more you will become tangled up in the yoke of the Law.

Paul concludes the whole matter with the above statement. "You want to be justified by the Law, by circumcision, and by works. We cannot see it. To be justified by such means would make Christ of no value to us. We would be obliged to perform the whole law. We rather through the Spirit wait for the hope of righteousness."

This is sweet comfort for us.

Your righteousness rests on something much better than feelings. Wait and hope until it will be revealed to you in the Lord's own time. Don't go by your feelings, but go by the doctrine of faith, which pledges Christ to you.

> *Don't go by your feelings, but go by the doctrine of faith, which pledges Christ to you.*

You may say, "The trouble is I don't feel as if I am righteous." You must not feel, but believe. Unless you believe that you are righteous, you do Christ a great wrong, for He has cleansed you by the washing of regeneration, He died for you so that through Him you may obtain righteousness and everlasting life.

Faith Working Through Love

Faith must of course be sincere. It must be a faith that performs good works through love. If faith lacks love it is not true faith.

He declares on the one hand, "In Christ Jesus circumcision availeth nothing," i.e., works avail nothing, but faith alone, and that without any merit whatever, avails before God. On the other hand, the Apostle declares that without fruits faith serves no purpose. To think, "If faith justifies without works, let us work nothing," is to despise the grace of God. Idle faith is not justifying faith. In this terse manner Paul presents the whole life of a Christian. Inwardly it consists in faith towards God, outwardly in love towards our fellow-men.

You were running well. Who hindered you from obeying the truth? This persuasion is not from him who calls you. A little leaven leavens the whole lump. I have confidence in the Lord that you will take no other view, and the one who is troubling you will bear the penalty, whoever he is. But if I, brothers, still preach circumcision, why am I still being persecuted? In that case the offense of the cross has been removed. I wish those who unsettle you would emasculate themselves! - Galatians 5:7-12 (ESV)

Paul compares the Christian life to a race. When everything runs along smoothly the Hebrews spoke of it as a race. "Ye did run well," means that everything went along smoothly and happily with the Galatians. They lived a Christian life and were on the right way to everlasting life. The words, "Ye did run well," are encouraging indeed. Often our lives seem to creep rather than to run. But if we abide in the true doctrine and walk in the spirit, we have nothing to worry about. God judges our lives differently. What may seem to us a life slow in Christian development may seem to God a life of rapid progression in grace.

The Galatians were hindered in the Christian life when they turned from faith and grace to the Law. Covertly the Apostle blames the false apostles for impeding the Christian progress of the Galatians. The false apostles persuaded the Galatians to believe that they were in error and that they had made little or no progress under the influence of Paul.

The devil is a cunning persuader. He knows how to enlarge the smallest sin into a mountain until we think we have committed the worst crime ever committed on earth. Such stricken consciences must be comforted and set straight as Paul corrected the Galatians by showing them that their opinion is not of Christ because it runs counter to the Gospel, which describes Christ as a meek and merciful Savior.

To those that are cast down on account of their sins Christ must be introduced as a Savior and Gift, and not as an example. But to sinners who live in a false assurance, Christ must be introduced as an example.

The Crazy Ones

Some may be tempted to call the Christians crazy. Deliberately to court danger by preaching and confessing the truth, and thus to bring upon ourselves the hatred and enmity of the whole world, is this not madness? But Paul does not mind the enmity of the world. It made him all the bolder to confess Christ. The enmity of the world in his estimation augurs well for the success and growth of the Church, which fares best in times of persecution. When the offense of the Cross ceases, when the rage of the enemies of the Cross abates, when everything is quiet, it is a sign that the devil is the door-keeper of the Church and that the pure doctrine of God's Word has been lost.

Persecution always follows on the heels of the Word of God as the Psalmist experienced. "I believe, therefore have I spoken: I was greatly afflicted." (Ps. 116:10.)

The Christians are accused and slandered without mercy. Murderers and thieves receive better treatment than Christians. The world regards true Christians as the worst offenders, for whom no punishment can be too severe. The world hates the Christians with amazing brutality, and without compunction commits them to the most shameful death, congratulating itself that it has rendered God and the cause of peace a distinct service by ridding the world of the undesired presence of these Christians. We are not to let such treatment cause us to falter in our adherence to Christ. As long as we experience such persecutions we know all is well with the Gospel.

So do not be surprised or offended when hell breaks loose. Look upon it as a happy indication that all is well with the Gospel of the Cross. God forbid that the offense of the Cross should ever be removed. This would be the case if we were to preach what the prince of this world and his followers would be only too glad to hear, the righteousness of works.

The Doctrine of Good Works

Now come all kinds of admonitions and precepts. It was the custom of the apostles that after they had taught faith and instructed the conscience they followed it up with admonitions unto good works, that the believers might manifest the duties of love toward each other. In order to avoid the appearance as if Christianity militated against good works or opposed civil government, the Apostle also urges us to give ourselves unto good works, to lead an honest life, and to keep faith and love with one another. This will give the lie to the accusations of the world that we Christians are the enemies of decency and of public peace. The fact is we Christians know better what constitutes a truly good work than all the philosophers and legislators of the world because we link believing with doing.

For you were called to freedom, brothers. Only do not use your freedom as an opportunity for the flesh, but through love serve one another. For the whole law is fulfilled in one word: "You shall love your neighbor as yourself." But if you bite and devour one another, watch out that you are not consumed by one another. - Galatians 5:13-15 (ESV)

In other words: "You have gained liberty through Christ, i.e., You are above all laws as far as conscience is concerned. You are saved. Christ is your liberty and life. Therefore law, sin, and death may not hurt you or drive you to despair. This is the constitution of your priceless liberty. Now take care that you do not use your wonderful liberty for an occasion of the flesh."

Satan likes to turn this liberty which Christ has gotten for us into licentiousness.

Now take care that you do not use your wonderful liberty for an occasion of the flesh.

This attitude is common enough. People talk about Christian liberty and then go and cater to the desires of covetousness, pleasure, pride, envy, and other vices. Nobody wants to fulfill his duties. Nobody wants to help out a brother in distress. This sort of thing makes me so impatient at times that I wish the swine who trampled precious pearls under foot were back once again under the tyranny of the Pope. You cannot wake up the people of Gomorrah with the gospel of peace.

Even we creatures of the world do not perform our duties as zealously in the light of the Gospel as we did before in the darkness of ignorance, because the surer we are of the liberty purchased for us by Christ, the more we neglect the Word, prayer, well-doing, and suffering. If Satan were not continually molesting us with trials, with the persecution of our enemies, and the ingratitude of our brethren, we would become so careless and indifferent to all good works that in time we would lose our faith in Christ, resign the ministry of the Word, and look for an easier life. Many of our ministers are beginning to do that very thing. They complain about the ministry, they maintain they cannot live on their salaries, they whimper about the miserable treatment they receive at the hand of those whom they delivered from the servitude of the law by the preaching of the Gospel. These ministers desert our poor and maligned Christ, involve themselves in the affairs of the world, seek advantages for themselves and not for Christ.

In order that Christians may not abuse their liberty the Apostle encumbers them with the rule of mutual love that they should serve each other in love. Let everybody perform the duties of his station and vocation diligently and help his neighbor to the limit of his capacity.

Christians are glad to hear and obey this teaching of love. When others hear about this Christian liberty of ours they at once infer, "If I am free, I may do what I like. If salvation is not a matter of doing why should we do anything for the poor?" In this crude manner they turn the liberty of the spirit into wantonness and licentiousness. We want them to know, however, that if they use their lives and possessions after their own pleasure, if they do not help the poor, if they cheat their fellow-men in business and snatch and scrape by hook and by crook everything they can lay their hands on, we want to tell them that they are not free, no matter how much they think they are, but they are the dirty slaves of the devil.

As for us, we are obliged to preach the Gospel which offers to all men liberty from the Law, sin, death, and God's wrath. We have no right to conceal or revoke this liberty proclaimed by the Gospel.

And so we cannot do anything with the swine who dive headlong into the filth of licentiousness. We do what we can, we diligently admonish them to love and to help their fellow-men. If our admonitions bear no fruit, we leave them to God, who will in His own good time take care of these disrespecters of His goodness. In the meanwhile we comfort ourselves with the thought that our labors are not lost upon the true believers. They appreciate this spiritual liberty and stand ready to serve others in love and, though their number is small, the satisfaction they give us far outweighs the discouragement which we receive at the hands of the large number of those who misuse this liberty.

Upon this foundation the Apostle erects the structure of good works which he defines in this one sentence: "Thou shalt love thy neighbour as thyself."

In adding such precepts of love the Apostle embarrasses the false apostles very much, as if he were saying to the Galatians: "I have described to you what spiritual life is. Now I will also teach you what truly good works are. I am doing this in order that you may understand that the silly ceremonies of which the false apostles make so much are far inferior to the works of Christian love." This is the hall-mark of all false teachers, that they not only pervert the pure doctrine but also fail in doing good. Their foundation vitiated, they can only build wood, hay, and stubble. Oddly enough, the false apostles who were such earnest champions of good works never required the work of charity, such as Christian love and the practical charity of a helpful tongue, hand, and heart. Their only requirement was that circumcision, days, months, years, and times should be observed. They could not think of any other good works.

The Apostle exhorts all Christians to practice good works after they have embraced the pure doctrine of faith, because even though they have been justified they still have the old flesh to refrain them from doing good. Therefore it becomes necessary that sincere preachers cultivate the doctrine of good works as diligently as the doctrine of faith, for Satan is a deadly enemy of both.

Paul knows how to explain the law of God. He condenses all the laws of Moses into one brief sentence. Reason takes offense at the brevity with which Paul treats the Law. Therefore reason looks down upon the doctrine of faith and its truly good works. To serve one another in love, i.e., to instruct the erring, to comfort the afflicted, to raise the fallen, to help one's neighbor in every possible way, to bear with his infirmities, to endure hardships, toil, ingratitude in the Church and in the world, and on the other hand to obey government, to honor one's parents, to be patient at home with a nagging wife and an unruly family, these things are not at all regarded as good works. The fact is, they are such excellent works that the world cannot possibly estimate them at their true value.

Even though they have been justified they still have the old flesh to refrain them from doing good.

It is tersely spoken: "Love thy neighbour as thyself." But what more needs to be said? You cannot find a better or nearer example than your own. If you want to know how you ought to love your neighbor, ask yourself how much you love yourself. If you were to get into trouble or danger, you would be glad to have the love and help of all men. You do not need any book of instructions to teach you how to love your neighbor. All you have to do is to look into your own heart, and it will tell you how you ought to love your neighbor as yourself.

My neighbor is every person, especially those who need my help, as Christ explained in the tenth chapter of Luke. Even if a person has done me some wrong, or has hurt me in any way, he is still a human being with flesh and blood. As long as a person remains a human being, so long is he to be an object of our love.

If you are so anxious to do good works, I will tell you in one word how you can fulfill all laws. 'By love serve one another.' You will never lack people to whom you may do good. The world is full of people who need your help."

It is not an easy matter to teach faith without works, and still to require works. Unless the ministers of Christ are wise in handling the mysteries of God and rightly divide the word, faith and good works may easily be confused. Both the doctrine of faith and the doctrine of good works must be diligently taught, and yet in such a way that both the doctrines stay within their God-given sphere. If we only teach works, as our opponents do, we shall lose the faith. If we only teach faith people will come to think that good works are superfluous.

But I say, walk by the Spirit, and you will not gratify the desires of the flesh. For the desires of the flesh are against the Spirit, and the desires of the Spirit are against the flesh, for these are opposed to each other, to keep you from doing the things you want to do. But if you are led by the Spirit, you are not under the law. Now the works of the flesh are evident: sexual immorality, impurity, sensuality, idolatry, sorcery, enmity, strife, jealousy, fits of anger, rivalries, dissensions, divisions, envy, drunkenness, orgies, and things like these. I warn you, as I warned you before, that those who do such things will not inherit the kingdom of God. - Galatians 5:16-21 (ESV)

The lust of the flesh is not altogether extinct in us. It rises up again and again and wrestles with the Spirit. No flesh, not even that of the true believer, is so completely under the influence of the Spirit that it will not bite or devour, or at least neglect, the commandment of love. At the slightest provocation it flares up, demands to be revenged, and hates a neighbor like an enemy, or at least does not love him as much as he ought to be loved.

Therefore the Apostle establishes this rule of love for the believers. Serve one another in love. Bear the infirmities of your brother. Forgive one another. Without such bearing and forbearing, giving and forgiving, there can be no unity because to give and to take offense are unavoidably human.

Whenever you are angry with your brother for any cause, repress your violent emotions through the Spirit. Bear with his weakness and love him. He does not cease to be your neighbor or brother because he offended you. On the contrary, he now more than ever before requires your loving attention.

The scholastics take the lust of the flesh to mean carnal lust. True, believers too are tempted with carnal lust. Even the married are not immune to carnal lusts. Men set little value upon that which they have and covet what they have not, as the poet says:

"The things most forbidden we always desire, And things most denied we seek to acquire."

Do not despair if you feel the flesh battling against the Spirit or if you cannot make it behave. For you to follow the guidance of the Spirit in all things without interference on the part of the flesh is impossible. You are doing all you can if you resist the flesh and do not fulfill its demands.

When I was a monk I thought I was lost forever whenever I felt an evil emotion, carnal lust, wrath, hatred, or envy. I tried to quiet my conscience in many ways, but it did not work, because lust would always come back and give me no rest. I told myself: "You have permitted this and that sin, envy, impatience, and the like. Your joining this holy order has been in vain, and all your good works are good for nothing." If at that time I had understood this passage, "The flesh lusteth against the Spirit, and the Spirit against the flesh," I could have spared myself many a day of self-torment. I would have said to myself: "Martin, you will never be without sin, for you have flesh. Despair not, but resist the flesh."

No man is to despair of salvation just because he is aware of the lust of the flesh. Let him be aware of it so long as he does not yield to it. The passion of lust, wrath, and other vices may shake him, but they are not to get him down. Sin may assail him, but he is not to welcome it. Yes, the better Christian a man is, the more he will experience the heat of the conflict. This explains the many expressions of regret in the Psalms and in the entire Bible. Everybody is to determine his peculiar weakness and guard against it. Watch and wrestle in spirit against your weakness. Even if you cannot completely overcome it, at least you ought to fight against it.

The better Christian a man is,
the more he will experience the heat of the conflict.

Paul does not enumerate all the works of the flesh, but only certain ones. First, he mentions various kinds of carnal lusts, as adultery, fornication, wantonness, etc. But carnal lust is not the only work of the flesh, and so he counts among the works of the flesh also idolatry, witchcraft, hatred, and the like.

Idolatry
The best religion, the most fervent devotion without Christ is plain idolatry. It has been considered a holy act when the monks in their cells meditate upon God and His works, and in a religious frenzy kneel down to pray and to weep for joy. Yet Paul calls it simply idolatry. Every religion which worships God in ignorance or neglect of His Word and will is idolatry.

Witchcraft
Witchcraft is a brand of idolatry. As witches used to bewitch cattle and men, so idolaters, i.e., all the self-righteous, go around to bewitch God and to make Him out as one who justifies men not by grace through faith in Christ but by the works of men's own choosing. They bewitch and deceive themselves.

Sects
Under sects Paul here understands heresies. Heresies have always been found in the church. What unity of faith can exist among all the different monks and the different orders? None whatever. There is no unity of spirit, no agreement of minds, but great dissension. There is no conformity in doctrine, faith, and life. On the other hand, among evangelical Christians the Word, faith, religion, sacraments, service, Christ, God, heart, and mind are common to all. This unity is not disturbed by outward differences of station or of occupation.

Drunkenness, Gluttony
Paul does not say that eating and drinking are works of the flesh, but intemperance in eating and drinking, which is a common vice

nowadays, is a work of the flesh. Those who are given to excess are to know that they are not spiritual but carnal.

"Those who do such things will not inherit the kingdom of God."

This is a hard saying, but very necessary for those false Christians and hypocrites who speak much about the Gospel, about faith, and the Spirit, yet live after the flesh. But this hard sentence is directed chiefly at the heretics who are large with their own self-importance, that they may be frightened into taking up the fight of the Spirit against the flesh.

> *But the fruit of the Spirit is love, joy, peace, patience, kindness, goodness, faithfulness, gentleness, self-control; against such things there is no law. And those who belong to Christ Jesus have crucified the flesh with its passions and desires.*
>
> *If we live by the Spirit, let us also keep in step with the Spirit. Let us not become conceited, provoking one another, envying one another. - Galatians 5:22-26 (ESV)*

The Apostle does not speak of the works of the Spirit as he spoke of the works of the flesh, but he attaches to these Christian virtues a better name. He calls them the fruits of the Spirit.

Love
It would have been enough to mention only the single fruit of love, for love embraces all the fruits of the Spirit.

Joy
Joy means sweet thoughts of Christ, melodious hymns and psalms, praises and thanksgiving, with which Christians instruct, inspire, and refresh themselves.

Peace
Peace towards God and men. Christians are to be peaceful and quiet. Not argumentative, not hateful, but thoughtful and patient.

Longsuffering

Longsuffering is that quality which enables a person to bear adversity, injury, reproach, and makes them patient to wait for the improvement of those who have done him wrong. When the devil finds that he cannot overcome certain persons by force he tries to overcome them in the long run. He knows that we are weak and cannot stand anything long.

Gentleness

Gentleness in conduct and life. True followers of the Gospel must not be sharp and bitter, but gentle, mild, courteous, and soft-spoken, which should encourage others to seek their company. Gentleness can overlook other people's faults and cover them up. Gentleness is always glad to give in to others.

Goodness

A person is good when he is willing to help others in their need.

Faith

In listing faith among the fruits of the Spirit, Paul obviously does not mean faith in Christ, but faith in men. Such faith is not suspicious of people but believes the best. Naturally the possessor of such faith will be deceived, but he lets it pass.

Meekness

A person is meek when he is not quick to get angry. Many things occur in daily life to provoke a person's anger, but the Christian gets over his anger by meekness.

Temperance

Christians are to lead sober and chaste lives. They should not be adulterers, fornicators, or sensualists. They should not be quarrelers or drunkards.

A Word to Preachers

The Gospel is not there for us to aggrandize ourselves. The Gospel is to aggrandize Christ and the mercy of God. It holds out to men eternal gifts that are not gifts of our own manufacture. What right have we to receive praise and glory for gifts that are not of our own making?

The ministers of the Gospel should be men who are not too easily affected by praise or criticism, but simply speak out the benefit and the glory of Christ and seek the salvation of souls.

Whenever you are being praised, remember it is not you who is being praised but Christ, to whom all praise belongs. When you preach the Word of God in its purity and also live accordingly, it is not your own doing, but God's doing. And when people praise you, they really mean to praise God in you. When you understand this--and you should because "what hast thou that thou didst not receive?"--you will not flatter yourself on the one hand and on the other hand you will not carry yourself with the thought of resigning from the ministry when you are insulted, reproached, or persecuted.

It is really kind of God to send so much infamy, reproach, hatred, and cursing our way to keep us from getting proud of the gifts of God in us. We need a millstone around our neck to keep us humble. There are a few on our side who love and revere us for the ministry of the Word, but for every one of these there are a hundred on the other side who hate and persecute us.

Good works may improve
the outward appearance,
but they cannot produce a
new creature.

Martin Luther

A Gospel Farewell
Chapter 6

Brothers and sisters, if someone is caught in a sin, you who live by the Spirit should restore that person gently. But watch yourselves, or you also may be tempted. Carry each other's burdens, and in this way you will fulfill the law of Christ. If anyone thinks they are something when they are not, they deceive themselves. Each one should test their own actions. Then they can take pride in themselves alone, without comparing themselves to someone else, for each one should carry their own load. Nevertheless, the one who receives instruction in the word should share all good things with their instructor.

Do not be deceived: God cannot be mocked. A man reaps what he sows. Whoever sows to please their flesh, from the flesh will reap destruction; whoever sows to please the Spirit, from the Spirit will reap eternal life. Let us not become weary in doing good, for at the proper time we will reap a harvest if we do not give up. Therefore, as we have opportunity, let us do good to all people, especially to those who belong to the family of believers. - Galatians 6:1-10 (NIV)

The Apostle takes the authors of sects to task for being hard-hearted tyrants. They despise the weak and demand that everything be just so. Nothing suits them except what they do. Unless you eulogize whatever they say or do, unless you adapt yourself to their slightest whim, they become angry with you. They are that way because, as St. Paul says, they "think themselves to be something," they think they know all about the Scriptures.

Paul has their number when he calls them zeros. They deceive themselves with their self-suggested wisdom and holiness. They have no understanding of Christ or the law of Christ. By insisting that everything be perfect they not only fail to bear the burdens of the weak, they actually offend the weak by their severity. People begin to hate and shun them and refuse to accept counsel or comfort from them.

Paul describes these stiff and ungracious saints accurately when he says of them, "They think themselves to be something." Bloated by their own silly ideas and schemes they entertain a pretty fair opinion of themselves, when in reality they amount to nothing.

The Gospel & Persecution
The Gospel entails persecution. The Gospel is that kind of a doctrine. Furthermore, the disciples of the Gospel are not all dependable. Many embrace the Gospel today and tomorrow discard it. To preach the Gospel for praise is bad business especially when people stop praising you. Find your praise in the testimony of a good conscience.

This passage may also be applied to other work besides the ministry. When an official, a servant, a teacher minds his business and performs his duty faithfully without concerning himself about matters that are not in his line he may rejoice in himself. The best commendation of any work is to know that one has done the work that God has given him well and that God is pleased with his effort.

That means: For anybody to covet praise is foolish because the praise of men will be of no help to you in the hour of death. Before the judgment throne of Christ everybody will have to bear his own burden. As it is the praise of men stops when we die. Before the eternal Judge it is not praise that counts but your own conscience.

True, the consciousness of work well done cannot quiet the conscience. But it is well to have the testimony of a good conscience in the last judgment that we have performed our duty faithfully in accordance with God's will.

The Apostle intends soon to close his Epistle and therefore repeats once more the general exhortation unto good deeds. He means to say "Let us do good not only to the ministers of the Gospel, but to everybody, and let us do it without weariness." It is easy enough to do good once or twice, but to keep on doing good without getting disgusted with the ingratitude of those whom we have benefited, that is not so easy. Therefore the Apostle does not only admonish us to do good, but to do good untiringly. For our encouragement he adds the promise: "For in due season we shall reap, if we faint not." "Wait for the harvest and then you will reap the reward of your sowing to the Spirit. Think of that when you do good and the ingratitude of men will not stop you from doing good."

See what large letters I use as I write to you with my own hand! Those who want to impress people by means of the flesh are trying to compel you to be circumcised. The only reason they do this is to avoid being persecuted for the cross of Christ. Not even those who are circumcised keep the law, yet they want you to be circumcised that they may boast about your circumcision in the flesh. May I never boast except in the cross of our Lord Jesus Christ, through which the world has been crucified to me, and I to the world. Neither circumcision nor uncircumcision means anything; what counts is the new creation. Peace and mercy to all who follow this rule—to the Israel of God. From now on, let no one cause me trouble, for I bear on my body the marks of Jesus. - Galatians 6:11-17 (NIV)

Paul once more scores the false apostles in an effort to draw the Galatians away from their false doctrine. "The teachers you have now do not seek the glory of Christ and the salvation of your souls, but only their own glory. They avoid the Cross. They do not understand what they teach."

In other words: "I shall tell you what kind of teachers you have now. They avoid the Cross, they teach no certain truths. They think they are performing the Law, but they are not. They have not the Holy Spirit and without Him nobody can keep the Law." Where the Holy Ghost does not dwell in men there dwells an unclean spirit, a spirit that despises God and turns every effort at keeping the Law into a double sin.

Mark what the Apostle is saying: Those who are circumcised do not fulfill the Law. No self-righteous person ever does. To work, pray, or suffer apart from Christ is to work, pray, and to suffer in vain, "for whatsoever is not of faith is sin." It does a person no good to be circumcised, to fast, to pray, or to do anything, if in his heart he despises Christ.

To work, pray, or suffer apart from Christ
is to work, pray, and to suffer in vain

The New Creature

However, we learn from the Word of God that there is nothing under the sun that can make us righteous before God and a new creature except Christ Jesus.

A new creature is one in whom the image of God has been renewed. Such a creature cannot be brought into life by good works, but by Christ alone. Good works may improve the outward appearance, but they cannot produce a new creature. A new creature is the work of the Holy Ghost, who imbues our hearts with faith, love, and other Christian virtues, grants us the strength to subdue the flesh and to reject the righteousness of the world.

This is the rule by which we ought to live, "that ye put on the new man, which after God is created in righteousness and true holiness." (Eph. 4:24.) Those who walk after this rule enjoy the favor of God, the forgiveness of their sins, and peace of conscience. Should they ever be overtaken by any sin, the mercy of God supports them.

The Apostle speaks these words with a certain amount of indignation. "I have preached the Gospel to you in conformity with the revelation which I received from Jesus Christ. If you do not care for it, very well. Trouble me no more. Trouble me no more."

The grace of our Lord Jesus Christ be with your spirit, brothers and sisters. Amen. - Galatians 6:18 (NIV)

This is the Apostle's farewell. He ends his Epistle as he began it by wishing the Galatians the grace of God. We can hear him say: "I have presented Christ to you, I have pleaded with you, I have reproved you, I have overlooked nothing that I thought might be of benefit to you. All I can do now is to pray that our Lord Jesus Christ would bless my Epistle and grant you the guidance of the Holy Ghost."

The Lord Jesus Christ, our Savior, who gave me the strength and the grace to explain this Epistle and granted you the grace to hear it, preserve and strengthen us in faith unto the day of our redemption. To Him, the Father and the Son and the Holy Spirit, be glory, world without end.

Amen.

Editor Biography

I'm RJ Grunewald and I love getting to do what God has called me to do. I'm a husband to my wonderful wife, Jessica, and a dad to our son Elijah and our daughter Emaline. I also have the privilege to serve at the church my wife and I have grown up at, Faith Lutheran Church in Troy, Michigan. I serve in our student ministry and our on preaching team. I am currently attending Concordia Seminary in St. Louis, Missouri through their Specific Ministry Pastor program.

I write all the time about theology for everyday life, you can find out more about my writing at *www.rjgrune.com.*

Made in the USA
San Bernardino, CA
31 May 2017